REACHING OUT

interpersonal effectiveness
and
self-actualization

DAVID W. JOHNSON

University of Minnesota

Prentice-Hall, Inc., Englewood Cliffs, New Jersey

*To my brothers and sisters, who have significantly contributed
to the development of my interpersonal skills
and to my self-actualization:*
Frank, Helen, Roger, Edythe, Keith, Dale

© 1972 by Prentice-Hall, Inc., Englewood Cliffs, New Jersey

ISBN: P 0-13-753269-5
C 0-13-753277-6

Library of Congress Catalog Card Number: 77-38799

Printed in the United States of America

19   18   17   16   15   14   13

PRENTICE-HALL INTERNATIONAL, INC., *London*
PRENTICE-HALL OF AUSTRALIA, PTY. LTD., *Sydney*
PRENTICE-HALL OF CANADA, LTD., *Toronto*
PRENTICE-HALL OF INDIA PRIVATE LIMITED, *New Delhi*
PRENTICE-HALL OF JAPAN, INC., *Tokyo*

Contents

Preface

Reaching Out seeks to provide the theory and experiences necessary to develop effective interpersonal skills. It is more than a book of exercises; the theory presented places the exercises within a context that will give meaning to the reader's experiences in participating in the exercises.

"PROJECT YOUTH"

Much of the material in this book was developed for a project of the Youth Research Center, Minneapolis, Minnesota funded by the National Institute of Mental Health (MH 17615-02, Merton P. Strommen, Principal Investigator) known as *Project Youth—Youth Reaching Youth*. Some of the readers of this book will be using it for the purposes outlined by *Project Youth;* this foreword is specifically for them. *Project Youth* was founded to answer the question, "Can a portion of our nation's youth be trained to help those who seem to be headed for a life of unhappiness, delinquency, and general tragedy?" It hypothesized that youth and young adults could be taught to identify lonely and alienated peers and to establish friendships with them. It was based on the assumptions that (1) there are many lonely young people who never seek adult help for their personal problems and unhappiness but who are receptive to the support and friendship of a person their own age and (2) the human qualities of warmth, genuineness, and rapport can supply a missing and important part in the lives of many of the alienated and lonely young people in our society today. The material in this book can be and has been used for programs aimed at training young people to reach out and help those of their peers who are headed for personal difficulties and to alter their behavior and lives by becoming their friends.

For readers participating in programs similar to *Project Youth* this book will help you increase your skills in initiating friendships with others, especally with others who are at the moment lonely and isolated. For those of us who have several good friends, friendships and good relationships may not seem vital and important. As long as you are involved in meaningful relationships you may be unaware of how important they are. But for someone without a single close friend, making a personal friend may be the most important thing that has ever happened. For someone who feels that no one values him, that no one will support him when he needs support, that there is no one he can talk to when he feels troubled or to laugh with when he feels joy, life is a very lonely and sad business. A great deal of evidence indicates that in order to stay psychologically healthy a person has to have good relationships with other individuals. One of the most important things you, the reader, can do, therefore, is to reach out and initiate friendships with individuals who now do not seem to have other friends.

Besides learning the skills involved in initiating new friendships, this book will help you increase your skills in maintaining good relationships over time. When a friend asks you for help, for example, what is the best way to respond? When a friend is going through a personal or family crisis and needs your support and you want to express your concern, how may you best do it? Do you often feel helpless when someone needs your help and support? Do you often feel speechless when you want to express your concern and affection for another person? This book is aimed· at providing you with increased skills in helping your friends, showing concern, support, and affection, and in maintaining a good relationship with another person.

Look around you at school, at your job, and on the street. The world is full of lonely people to whom the development of a friendship may be the most important thing that has ever happened. The activities you will engage in to develop the skills emphasized in this book will often be fun and playful, but the application of these skills to real relationships is a serious concern. Through learning the skills involved in initiating and maintaining a friendship with another person you, the reader, may become the most meaningful and positive person in another individual's life.

ACKNOWLEDGMENTS

I need to thank many people for their help in writing this book. My younger sister, Edythe Johnson, contributed most of the questions the reader will find in the text. I have tried to acknowledge sources of the exercises in the book whenever possible. Some of the exercises presented are so commonly used that the originators are not traceable. If I have inadvertently missed giving recognition to anyone, I apologize. The staff of the Youth Research Center, especially Marilyn Graves and Mary Kay O'Brien, were very helpful in facilitating my work on the manuscript. Earlier drafts of much of the manuscript were used by Elaine Allen, Barbara Holm, Dale Joel, Paula McClung, Ann Mikkelson, Rondi Olson, Mark Quesnel, Isabelle Robinson, Pam Rossow, Dave Severson, Bruce Stone, Thomas Kretscher, and one hundred and fifty teenagers—all of whom were involved in *Project Youth*. Their helpful suggestions for revisions are appreciated. Finally, I would like to thank all those individuals who have participated in various types of laboratory-training experiences with me and have facilitated my growth as a person and a professional. All photos used in this book are from my personal file.

D. W. J.

The Importance of Interpersonal Skills

chapter 1

One of the most distinctive aspects of being alive is the potential for joy, fun, excitement, caring, warmth, and personal fulfillment in your relationships with other people. Making new friends, deepening ongoing relationships, even falling in love, depend upon your interpersonal skills. Much of human society and human action seems based upon the liking people have for each other. The words which name degrees of interpersonal attraction, such as *like, love, dislike,* and *hate,* are among the most frequently used words in the English language. Because man is a social animal, most of his happiness and fulfillment rests upon his ability to relate effectively to other humans. In addition, the foundations of all civilizations rest upon man's ability to cooperate with other humans and to coordinate his actions with theirs. We are dependent upon other people for much of our personal happiness and fulfillment, and we must work effectively with other people in order to engage in our vocations and avocations competently. There is no way to overemphasize the importance of interpersonal skills in our lives.

What makes us human is the way in which we interact with other people. To the extent that our relationships reflect concern, friendship, love, caring, helping, kindness, and responsiveness we are becoming more human. To the extent that our relationships reflect the opposite of such qualities as these we are becoming more inhuman. It is the cruelty to and the destruction of other people that we label inhumane; it is the positive involvement with other people which we label humane.

Effective interpersonal skills do not just happen, nor do they appear magically; they are learned. The purpose of this book is to help you increase your skills in initiating, developing, and maintaining effective, fulfilling relationships with other people. For those of us whose work requires a great deal of interaction with other people (such as teachers, counselors, supervisors, social workers), the ability to relate to other individuals in productive and meaningful ways is a necessity. For those of us who feel that our growth and development as a person depend upon the quality of our personal friendships, the skills involved in creating such relationships are a necessity. This book is aimed at helping you to increase your interpersonal skills whether in order to improve your job performance or to find greater satisfaction in your friendships. Increasing those skills will also lead to an increasing capacity to be human.

SELF-ACTUALIZATION

The rapid technological change we have been experiencing for the past several decades has resulted in rapid cultural change within our society. Our culture seems to be changing from an emphasis on achievement to an emphasis upon self-actualization, from self-control to self-expression, from independence to interdependence, from endurance of stress to a capacity for joy, from full employment to full lives. The values of our society seem to be changing from an achievement-oriented, puritanical emphasis to a self-actualizing emphasis on the development of personal resources and the experiencing of joy and a sense of fulfillment in one's life. Mobility has become a hallmark of our society; the people we know and love today may be hundreds of miles away tomorrow. Several times in our lives we may be faced with beginning new relationships with a group of people whom we don't know. The ability to develop relationships which actualize our personal resources and in which we experience joy and a sense of fulfillment is becoming more and more crucial. The ability to initiate and terminate relationships is becoming more and more of a necessity.

Many psychologists believe that there is a drive for an organism to actualize its potentialities, that is, a drive towards self-actualization. Whether or not there is such a drive, it is apparent that self-actualization is an increasingly important concern for many people. Self-actualization consists primarily of being *time-competent,* that is, of having the ability to tie the past and the future to the present in meaningful continuity while fully living in the present. The self-actualized person appears to be less burdened by guilts, regrets, and resentments from the past than is the nonself-actualizing person, and his aspirations are tied meaningfully to present working goals.

Self-actualization is also dependent upon being autonomous. In order to understand autonomy it is necessary to differentiate between inner and other directedness. The *inner-directed person* adopted early in life a small number of values and principles which he rigidly adheres to no matter what the situation in which he finds himself is like. The *other-directed person* receives guidance and direction from the people he relates to; his behavior conforms rigidly to whatever is necessary to gain the approval of other people. The *autonomous person* is liberated from rigid adherence to parental values or to social pressures and expectancies. He flexibly applies his values and principles in order to behave in ways appropriate to the situations he is in.

The time-competence and the autonomy of the self-actualizing person are related in the sense that a person who lives primarily in the present relies more upon his own support and expressiveness than does a person living primarily in the past or in the future. To live fully in the present means that you must be autonomous of both rigid inner values and excessive needs to conform to social prescriptions to obtain approval from other people.

Self-actualization is achieved through relating to other people in time-competent and autonomous ways. A person's interpersonal skills are the foundation for his self-actualization. Whether we are aged 6, 16, or 60, the level of our interpersonal skills largely determines how effective and happy we are. In the following section the specific skills involved in creating self-actualizing relationships will be discussed.

INTERPERSONAL SKILLS

To initiate, develop, and maintain effective and fulfilling relationships certain basic skills must be present. These skills generally fall into four areas: (1) knowing and trusting each other, (2) accurately and unambiguously understanding each other, (3) influencing and helping each other, and (4) constructively resolving problems and conflicts in your relationship.

The first area of skill development involves self-disclosure, self-awareness, self-acceptance, and trust. There must be a high level of trust between you and the other person in order for you to get to know each other. Getting to know each other involves disclosing how you are reacting to and feeling about what is presently taking place. Such openness depends upon your self-awareness and your self-acceptance; if you are unaware of your feelings and reactions you cannot communicate them to another person and if you cannot accept your feelings and reactions you will try to hide them.

The second area of skill development focuses upon being able to communicate your ideas and feelings accurately and unambiguously. Especially important is the communication of warmth and liking. Unless you feel the other person likes you and he feels that you like him, a relationship will not grow.

When a friend asks you for help, what is the best way to respond? When someone you know is going through a personal or family crisis and needs your support, what is the best way to express your concern? The third area of skill development concerns mutual support and influence in the relationship. Responding in helpful ways to another person's problems and concerns, communicating acceptance and support, constructively confronting a friend, using reinforcement and modeling to influence another person's behavior are all important relationship skills.

Finally, learning how to resolve problems and conflicts in ways that bring you and the other person closer together and facilitate the growth and development of the relationship is vitally important to maintaining a relationship. Two chapters of this book therefore focus upon the constructive definition of interpersonal problems and the constructive management of interpersonal conflict.

THE APPLICATION OF BEHAVIORAL SCIENCE
RESEARCH TO INTERPERSONAL SKILLS

Relating to other individuals in effective and productive ways is a vital need of modern society. We have at our disposal a vast amount of behavioral science research on interpersonal dynamics. Yet this knowledge has not been translated into a form useful to individuals who wish to apply it to increase their interpersonal skills. This book aims to fill the gap between the findings of research on interpersonal interaction and the application of this knowledge to the development of interpersonal skills.

To make this book as readable as possible, however, a minimum of footnote references to research and theory are included. This does not mean that there is no empirical support for the behaviors recommended. The basic skills which determine a person's interpersonal effectiveness have been identified from the results of the author's research (Johnson, 1966, 1967, 1971a, 1971b, 1971c; Johnson and Dustin, 1970; Johnson and Lewicki, 1969), from the results of the research on effective therapeutic relationships (for example, Truax and Carkhuff, 1967; Bierman, 1969; Strupp and Bergin, 1969), and from the results of the social psychological research on interpersonal relationships (see Johnson, 1970, 1972; Watson and Johnson, 1972). In addition to the empirical evidence upon which the skills emphasized in this book are based, much of this book has been used in a training program which is being currently evaluated (see "Project Youth" foreword). Although it will be another two years before all the data gathered in this project have been analyzed, the early results indicate that the material in this book is quite effective in increasing the interpersonal skills of readers.

Any individual concerned with increasing his interpersonal skills, and any practitioners who work with other people, will find this book helpful. It is not a review of the theory and research for scholars. It translates the findings of theory and research on interpersonal relations into a program for developing the skills necessary for forming effective and fulfilling relationships with other people. Any individual, from a teenager to an elderly person, will be able to comprehend easily the material in this book.

CO-ORIENTATION

In building a relationship two individuals must be co-oriented; that is, they must operate under the same norms and adhere to the same values. The co-orientation does not have to be perfect; rewarding relationships are quite common between individuals from different cultures and different backgrounds. But in order to develop a relationship you must agree upon the norms and values which will determine your behavior in your relationship.

Norms refer to common expectations about the behavior appropriate for you and the other person in the relationship. Whether you ask each other to do favors, how personal your discussions are, what types of things you can depend upon each other for reflect the norms of the relationship. The norms of a relationship depend to a large extent upon the values the two individuals agree to adhere to in the relationship. The skills emphasized in this book will set norms about expected behavior in a relationship (that is, you should self-disclose, build trust, be supportive and accepting, try to help each other, and so on), and they are based upon a set of humanistic values (that is, you should assume responsibility for your ideas and feelings, strive towards self-actualization, engage in cooperative interaction, and have the capacity for intimate and personal relationships). Using the skills presented in your interaction with other people will promote norms which facilitate the development of effective and fulfilling relationships.

Often the establishment of mutual norms and values concerning how you and the other person are going to relate is more important than the actual technical interpersonal skills the two of you have. The mutual commitment to face differences and conflicts and resolve them constructively, for example, may be more important in facilitating the growth of the relationship than the actual technical skill you have for resolving conflicts constructively. Or the mutual commitment to be self-disclosing and genuine with each other may be more important in creating intimacy and comradeship than the actual skill with which you disclose your feelings and reactions. In this book the emphasis is placed upon developing your interpersonal skills. It should be remembered, however, that whenever you apply the skills discussed in this book you are also promoting a set of norms and values for your relationships. The mutual adoption of these norms and values may be more important in facilitating the development of effective and fulfilling relationships than the actual skill with which you apply the skills.

LEARNING NEW INTERPERSONAL SKILLS

There is a five-step process for learning a new skill:

1. Becoming aware of the need for and uses of a new skill.
2. Identifying the behaviors involved in the new skill.
3. Practicing the behaviors.
4. Receiving feedback concerning how well you are performing the behaviors.
5. Integrating the behaviors into your behavioral repertoire.

This book is designed to provide you with information concerning the nature of and the need for the interpersonal skills discussed. The behaviors involved in applying the skills will be specified. You will then be asked to answer questions to test your comprehension and understanding of the material presented. Next you will be given instructions for exercises that provide you with an opportunity to practice the behaviors and receive feedback concerning how well you are learning the behaviors. Often the exercises let you diagnose the present level of your skills. After engaging in the exercises it is up to you to practice the behaviors until you feel comfortable doing them. At the end of each chapter you will be asked to evaluate the extent to which you have mastered the skills presented.

While you practice the behaviors involved in the skills discussed, you may at first feel self-conscious and awkward. Practicing the behaviors may sometimes seem more like role-playing than genuine behavior. Do not let this stand in the way of increasing your interpersonal skills. It is through role-playing that most new skills are developed. If you keep practicing the behaviors, the self-consciousness and awkwardness will pass and you will become quite comfortable in using your increased skills.

A mechanical process is involved in specifying the behaviors that constitute a skill and in practicing them. While you engage in the exercises, you may at times feel the process is somewhat mechanical and unreal. But this is true of every kind of skill development. Learning how to play the piano, for example, also involves the mechanical practice of specific behaviors that seem unreal compared to the performance of a beautiful piano concerto. It is when you apply your new skills to real situations that they will gain the fire and life that may sometimes be lacking from practicing the exercises.

This book provides you with guidance for increasing your interpersonal skills. It is up to you to take advantage of the material and exercises presented and use it in ways which increase your interpersonal skills. The extent of your learning and skill development rests entirely upon your commitment to use the book in fruitful ways.

GROUP SUPPORT

In learning any new skills the approval of a group is a powerful source of motivation and support. Readers of this book may find it most rewarding to go through the exercises as part of a group. The group should consciously try to give approval to those members who are seriously trying to increase their interpersonal skills. The more a person practices and develops these skills the more group approval he should receive. By the same token, if a group supports member's attempts to experiment with new behavior and take risks in trying out their new skills, everyone's progress will be enhanced. There are few influences upon our behavior more powerful than the support and approval of a group of friends. Using the group influence to facilitate our learning is one of the most constructive ways of ensuring the development of our interpersonal skills.

Self-Disclosure

2

How well do I know myself? How well do other people know me? Am I an easy person to get to know? Do I feel free to tell others how I am reacting, feeling, and what I am thinking? These are important questions. To like you, to be involved with you, to be your friend, I must know who you are. In order for me to know you, you must know yourself. In order for you to feel free to disclose yourself to me, you must accept and appreciate yourself. In this chapter we will focus upon self-awareness and the disclosure of yourself to others. In a later chapter we will focus upon self-acceptance.

SELF-DISCLOSURE

Alienation from one's real self not only arrests one's growth as a person, it also tends to make a farce out of one's relationships with people. . . . A self-alienated person—one who does not disclose himself truthfully and fully—can never love another person nor can he be loved by another person. Effective loving calls for knowledge of the object. . . . How can I love a person whom I do not know? How can the other person love me if he does not know me? . . . A truly personal relationship between two people involves disclosure of self one to the other in full and spontaneous honesty. [S. Jourard, *The Transparent Self* (Princeton, N.J.: D. Van Nostrand Reinhold Co., 1964), pp. 25, 28.]

Without self-disclosure you cannot form a close personal relationship with another person. A relationship between two individuals develops

9

as the two become more open about themselves and more self-disclosing. If you cannot reveal yourself, you cannot become close to others, and you cannot be valued by others for who you are. To become closely involved with another person, you must know him and he must know you. Two people who share how they are reacting to situations and to each other are pulled together; two people who stay silent about their reactions and feelings stay strangers. To like you, to be involved with you, I must know who you are. To like me, to be involved with me, you must know who I am.

Self-disclosure may be defined as revealing how you are reacting to the present situation and giving any information about the past that is relevant to understanding how you are reacting to the present. Reactions to people and events are not facts as much as feelings. To be self-disclosing means to share with another person how you feel about something he has done or said, or how you feel about the events which have just taken place. Self-disclosure does not mean revealing intimate details of your past life. Making highly personal confessions about your past may lead to a temporary feeling of intimacy, but a relationship is built by disclosing your reactions to events you both experience or to what the other person says or does. A person comes to know and understand you not through knowing your past history but through knowing how you react. Past history is only helpful if it clarifies why you are reacting in a certain way.

There has been a considerable amount of research on the effects of self-disclosure upon interpersonal relationships (Johnson, 1972). There is, for example, much evidence that indicates that healthy relationships are based upon self-disclosure. If you hide how you are reacting to the other person, your concealment can sicken the relationship. The energy you pour into hiding adds to the stress of the relationship and dulls your awareness of your own inner experience, thus decreasing your ability to disclose your reactions even when it is perfectly safe and appropriate to do so. Hiding your reactions from others through fear of rejection and conflict or through feelings of shame and guilt leads to loneliness. Being silent is not being strong; strength is the willingness to take risks in the relationship, to disclose yourself with the intention of building a better relationship.

Several aspects of a relationship influence self-disclosure. The more self-disclosing you are to another person, the more likely that person will like you. You are more likely to self-disclose to a person you know and like than to a person you do not know or do not like. The amount of self-disclosure you engage in will influence the amount of self-disclosure the other person engages in; the more you self-disclose, the more the other person will tend to self-disclose.

Willingness to engage in self-disclosure is related to several characteristics. The research done in this field indicates that a person willing to be self-disclosing will likely be a competent, open, and socially extroverted person who feels a strong need to interact with others. He is likely to be flexible, adaptive, and perhaps more intelligent than his less self-revealing peers. He is objectively aware of the realities of the interpersonal situations in which he is involved and perceives a fairly close congruence between the way he is and the way in which he would like to be. Finally, he views his fellowman as generally good rather than evil.

Communicating intimately with another person, especially in times of stress, seems to be a basic human need. Disclosing yourself to another person builds a relationship which allows for such intimate communication, both by yourself and by the other. If neither you nor the other feels free to engage in self-disclosure, you can be of little or no help to each other during periods of stress.

Being self-disclosing means being "for real." It is important that your self-disclosures are as honest, genuine, and authentic as possible. In this chapter we will focus upon some of the skills involved in effective self-disclosure, but the communication of the sincerity, genuineness, and authenticity of your self-disclosures is one of the most important aspects of building a relationship.

In addition to being *open with* other people, you must be *open to* others to build meaningful relationships. Being open to another person means showing that you are interested in how he feels about what you are saying and doing. It is being receptive to his self-disclosure. This does not mean prying into the intimate areas of another's life. It means being willing to listen to his reactions to the present situation and to what you are doing and saying.

In responding to another's self-disclosure, it is important to accept and support him if possible. Being accepting and supportive will increase the other person's tendency to be open with you. It will strengthen the relationship and help it grow. Even when a person's behavior seriously offends you, it is possible for you to express acceptance of the person and disagreement with the way he behaves. To be open with another person is to risk rejection; to self-disclose is to ask for support and acceptance in trying to build a better relationship. You should be careful, therefore, to give the support and acceptance necessary for the relationship to grow.

REVELATION [1]

We make ourselves a place apart
Behind light words that tease and flout,

[1] From *The Poetry of Robert Frost,* edited by Edward Connery Lathem. Copyright 1934 by Holt, Rinehart and Winston, Inc. Copyright © 1962 by Robert Frost. Reprinted by permission of Holt, Rinehart and Winston, Inc., Jonathan Cape Ltd., the Estate of Robert Frost, and the editor.

But oh, the agitated heart
Til someone really finds us out.

Tis pity if the case requires
(or so we say) that in the end
We speak the literal to inspire
The understanding of a friend.

But so it is with babes at play
At hide and seek to guard afar.
So all who hide too well away
Must speak and tell us where they are.

—ROBERT FROST

You can test your understanding of this section by answering the following questions. Circle the correct answer. (Check yourself with the answer key found on p. 41.)

True False 1. Self-disclosure is revealing how you are reacting to the present and giving relevant information about the past.

True False 2. Self-disclosure helps a relationship grow.

True False 3. Self-disclosure means revealing the intimate details of your past life.

True False 4. Hiding your reactions to another person's behavior helps your relationship with that person grow.

True False 5. When a person's behavior seriously offends you, you should reject him as a person.

True False 6. Jim meets Mary at a party. Mary immediately begins to tell Jim about her relationship with her father. This is an example of self-disclosure.

True False 7. Communicating intimately with another person is a human need.

True False 8. Sandy and Bill are watching a sunset. Bill begins to explain to Sandy the way he is reacting to the sunset and goes into a childhood incident that has affected the way he reacts to sunsets. This is an example of self-disclosure.

True False 9. You should be self-disclosing at all times in all relationships.

APPROPRIATENESS OF SELF-DISCLOSURE

Self-disclosure must be relevant to your relationship with the other person and appropriate to the situation you are in. You can be too self-disclosing. A person who reveals too much of his reactions too fast may scare others away; a relationship is built gradually except in rare and special cases. Certainly being too self-disclosing will create as many relationship problems as disclosing too little. Although you should sometimes take risks with your self-disclosure to others, you should not be blind to the appropriateness of your behavior to the situation. Self-disclosure is appropriate when

1. It is not a random or isolated act but rather is part of an ongoing relationship.
2. It is reciprocated.
3. It concerns what is going on within and between persons in the present.
4. It creates a reasonable chance of improving the relationship.
5. Account is taken of the effect it will have upon the other person.
6. It is speeded up in a crisis in the relationship.
7. It gradually moves to a deeper level.

While relationships are built through self-disclosure, there are times when you will want to hide your reactions to the present situation from another person. If a person has clearly shown himself to be untrustworthy, it is foolish to be self-disclosing with him. If you know from past experience that the other person will misinterpret or overreact to your self-disclosure, you may wish to keep silent.

SELF-DISCLOSURE AND SELF-AWARENESS

Your ability to disclose yourself to others depends upon your self-awareness and self-acceptance. You must be aware of your reactions in order to communicate them to others. Without accepting your reactions you cannot feel free to allow other individuals to hear them. In this section we will focus upon self-awareness. In a later chapter in the book we will focus upon self-acceptance.

You should be continually trying to increase your self-awareness in order to be able to engage in self-disclosure. In order to discuss how you may increase your self-awareness, it may be helpful to look at the models found in Figures 2.1, 2.2, 2.3 (Luft, 1969).

These models are named the Johari Window after its two originators, Joe Luft and Harry Ingham. It illustrates that there are certain things you know about yourself and certain things that you do not know about yourself. Correspondingly, there are certain things other people know about you and certain things they do not know. It is assumed that it

FIGURE 2.1 IDENTIFICATION OF AREAS OF THE SELF

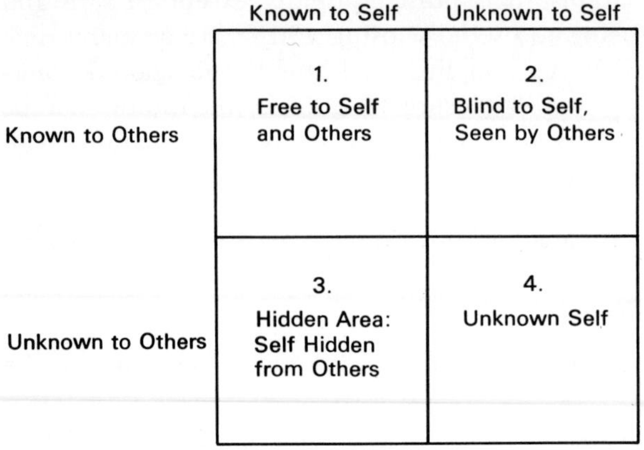

	Known to Self	Unknown to Self
Known to Others	1. Free to Self and Others	2. Blind to Self, Seen by Others
Unknown to Others	3. Hidden Area: Self Hidden from Others	4. Unknown Self

FIGURE 2.2 AT THE BEGINNING OF A RELATIONSHIP

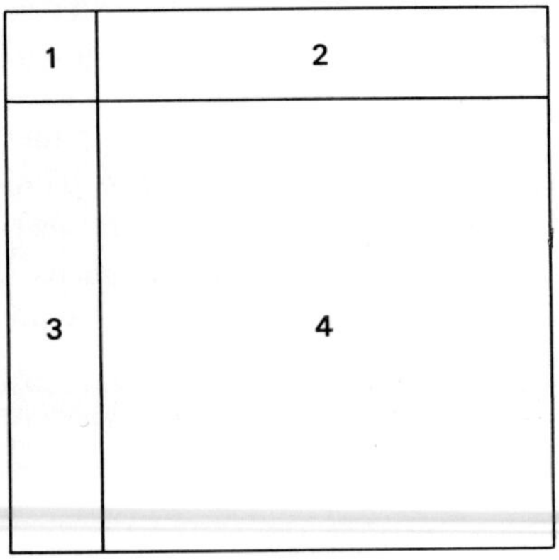

1	2
3	4

FIGURE 2.3 AFTER THE DEVELOPMENT OF A CLOSE RELATIONSHIP

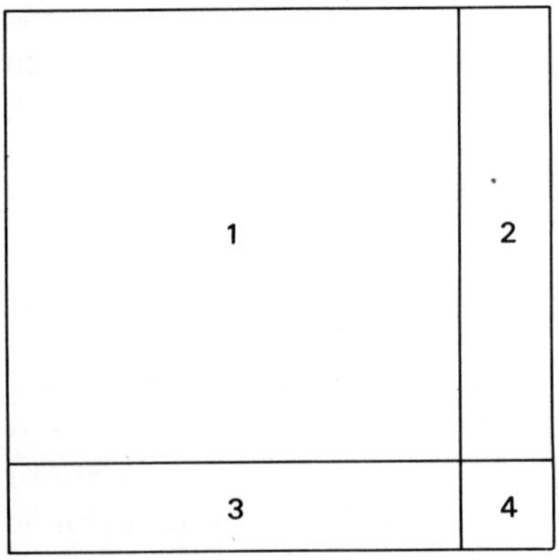

1	2
3	4

takes energy to hide information from yourself and others and that the more information that is known the clearer communication will be. Building a relationship therefore often involves working to enlarge the free area while decreasing the blind and hidden areas. As you become more self-disclosing, you reduce the hidden area. As you encourage others to be self-disclosing with you, your blind area is reduced. Through reducing your hidden area you give other people information to react to, which enables them to help you reduce your blind area. Through reducing your blind area, your self-awareness is increased; this helps you to be even more self-disclosing with others.

You can test your understanding of the Johari Window by answering the following questions. (Answers are on p. 41.)

1. Write "free," "hidden," "blind," or "unknown" in the appropriate space.

_____a. A boy is reluctant to express his resentment for another member of his group.

_____b. A girl does not know that both she and others think she is a critical person.

_____c. A boy expresses his religious doubts to his friends.

_____d. Unexpectedly, a girl expresses anger at a group she is a member of and cannot explain why she is angry.

2. The Johari Window illustrates (indicate the correct answer):
   a. Building a relationship involves enlarging your blind and hidden areas while decreasing your free areas.
   b. Building a relationship involves enlarging your free areas while decreasing your blind and hidden areas.
   c. Building a relationship involves opening your windows so other people can see you.

3. Look around at the members of your group. How large are your free areas with each of the other members? How large is each of their free areas with you?

FEEDBACK

Self-disclosing about how you are reacting to the way another person is behaving is often called *feedback*. The purpose of feedback is to provide constructive information to help another person become aware of how his behavior affects you and how you perceive his actions. It is important, therefore, to give feedback in a way which will not be threatening to the other person and increase his defensiveness. The more defensive an individual is, the less likely it is that he will correctly hear and understand feedback. Some characteristics of helpful, nonthreatening feedback are as follows:

1. *Focus feedback on behavior rather than the person.* It is important that you refer to what a person does rather than comment on what you imagine he is. To focus on behavior implies that you use adverbs (which relate to actions) rather than adjectives (which relate to qualities) when referring to a person. Thus you might say a person "talked considerably in this meeting," rather than that this person "is a loudmouth."

2. *Focus feedback on observations rather than inferences.* Observations refer to what you can see or hear in the behavior of another person, while inferences refer to interpretations and conclusions which you make from what you see or hear. In a sense, inferences or conclusions about a person contaminate your observations, thus clouding the feedback for another person. When inferences or conclusions are shared, and it may be valuable to do this, it is important that they be so identified.

3. *Focus feedback on description rather than judgment.* The effort to describe represents a process for reporting what occurred, while judgment refers to an evaluation in terms of good or bad, right or wrong, nice or not nice. Judgments arise out of a personal frame of reference or value system, whereas description represents *neutral* (as far as possible) reporting.

4. *Focus feedback on descriptions of behavior which are in terms of "more or less" rather than in terms of "either-or."* When you use "more or less" terminology, it implies that the behavior falls in a continuum. This means you are stressing quantity, which is objective and measurable, rather than quality, which is subjective and judgmental. Thus participation by a person may fall on a continuum from low participation to high participation, rather than "good" or "bad" participation. If you don't think in terms of more or less and the use of a continuous scale of measurement, you will be trapped into thinking in categories, which may then not reflect reality.

5. *Focus feedback on behavior related to a specific situation, preferably to the "here and now," rather than on behavior in the abstract, placing it in the "there and then."* What you and I do is always related in some way to time and place. We increase our understanding of behavior by keeping it tied to time and place. When observations or reactions occur, feedback will be most meaningful if you give it as soon as it is appropriate to do so.

6. *Focus feedback on the sharing of ideas and information rather than on giving advice.* By sharing ideas and information you leave the other person free to decide for himself, in the light of his own goals in a par-

ticular situation at a particular time, how to use the ideas and the information. When you give advice, you tell him what to do with the information. Insofar as you tell him what to do, you take away his freedom to determine for himself what is for him the most appropriate course of action.

7. *Focus feedback on exploration of alternatives rather than answers or solutions.* The more we can focus on a variety of procedures and means for accomplishing a particular goal, the less likely we are to accept premature answers or solutions—which may or may not fit a particular problem. Many of us have a collection of answers and solutions for which there are no problems.

8. *Focus feedback on the value it may have to the receiver, not on the value of "release" that it provides the person giving the feedback.* The feedback provided should serve the needs of the person getting the feedback rather than the needs of the giver. Help and feedback need to be given and heard as an offer, not as something you force upon another person.

9. *Focus feedback on the amount of information that the person receiving it can use, rather than on the amount that you have which you might like to give.* If you overload a person with feedback, it reduces the possibility that he may use what he receives effectively. When you give more than he can use, you are satisfying some need for yourself rather than helping the other person.

10. *Focus feedback on time and place so that personal data can be shared at appropriate times.* Because receiving and using personal feedback involves many possible emotional reactions, it is important for you to be sensitive to when it is appropriate to give feedback. Excellent feedback presented at an inappropriate time may do more harm than good. In short, the giving (and receiving) of feedback requires courage, skill, understanding, and respect for yourself and others.

11. *Focus feedback on what is said rather than why it is said.* When you relate feedback to the *what, how, when, where,* of what is said, you relate it to observable characteristics. If you relate feedback to why things are said, you go from the observable to the preferred, bringing up questions of "motive" or "content."

You may assess your understanding of feedback by answering the following questions. (Answers are on p. 41.)

1. You are giving feedback when you

_____a. Slap your date's face.

_____b. Self-disclose how you are reacting to the way another person is behaving.

_____c. React to what another person is doing.

_____d. Tell another person what is wrong with him.

2. The following are rules for constructive feedback:

True   False   a. Focus feedback on the person rather than upon his behavior.

True   False   b. Focus on inferences rather than observations.

True   False   c. Focus on description rather than judgment.

True   False   d. Focus on the "here and now" rather than upon the "there and then."

True   False   e. Focus on giving advice rather than sharing information.

True   False   f. Focus on what is said rather than upon why it is said.

True   False   g. Focus upon giving as much information as you can possibly think of rather than upon how much the other person can use.

INTERPERSONAL EFFECTIVENESS

The effectiveness of your behavior depends in large measure on your self-awareness; your self-awareness depends in large part upon receiving feedback from other individuals; the quality of the feedback you receive from other persons depends largely upon how much you self-disclose. In order to improve your interpersonal effectiveness you need to be aware of the consequences of your behavior and decide whether those consequences match your intentions. *Interpersonal effectiveness* can be defined as the degree to which the consequences of your behavior match your intentions.

When you interact with another person, you have no choice but to make some impact, stimulate some ideas, arouse some impressions and observations, or trigger some feelings and reactions. Sometimes you make the impression you want to, but at other times you may find that some people react to your behavior much differently than you would like them to. An expression of warmth, for instance, may be seen as your being condescending; an expression of anger may be seen as a joke. Your interpersonal effectiveness depends upon your ability to communicate clearly what you want to communicate, to create the impression you wish to, to influence the other person in the way you intend. You may improve your interpersonal effectiveness by self-disclosing your intentions, receiving feedback on your behavior, and modifying your behavior until other individuals perceive it as you mean it, that is, until it has the consequences you intend it to have.

EXERCISE IN INITIATING RELATIONSHIPS

The following exercise is a micro-experience in initiating relationships. The objectives of the exercise are as follows:

1. To initiate relationships with other individuals whom you do not know.
2. To share initial feelings and thoughts with other individuals.
3. To take risks in revealing yourself to other individuals.
4. To experience a variety of ways to disclose yourself to others.
5. To encourage openness, trust, risk-taking, and feedback with other individuals.

The activities are as follows:

1. Everyone stand up and mill around the room, making sure that you pass by everyone present. Greet each person nonverbally. This may be a handshake, a smile, a wink, a sock on the arm, or any other nonverbal way you may think of to say hello. After five minutes of milling, find a person you don't know. If you know everyone present, find the person you know least well.
2. Sit down with the person; each of you then take 2½ minutes to introduce yourself to the other. Do this by discussing the question of who you are as a person.
3. Turn around and find someone else near you whom you don't know or know least well of the other people present. Sit down with your new partner; each of you then take 2½ minutes to discuss the most significant experience you have had recently.
4. Find someone else you don't know. Sit down with your new partner and take five minutes (2½ minutes each) to exchange views on what you hope to accomplish by participating in this program.
5. Find another person whom you don't know. Sit down with your new partner and take five minutes (2½ minutes each) to share a fantasy or daydream that you often have. It may be connected with success, such as becoming President of the United States, or it may be connected with love, such as meeting a beautiful blonde who immediately falls in love with you, or it may be about what you would like to do with your next vacation.
6. Now form a group no larger than ten or twelve individuals. Try to be in a group with as many of the individuals as you have talked with in the previous activities. In the group discuss:

a. How you feel about the different members on the basis of the previous activities, first impressions, or past experience if you knew them previously.

b. Which activity you felt was most helpful in getting to know the person you were interacting with.

c. What you feel you have learned from this exercise.

d. What individuals in the group would need to share if you are to get to know them during this session.

e. Anything else that seems relevant to initiating relationships. This may continue for as long as you would like.

7. Alternative topics for discussion in pairs are these:
   a. What animal I would like to be and why.
   b. What song means the most to me and why.
   c. What it is that I like most about myself.
   d. How I would change myself if I had complete power to do so.
   e. My most significant childhood experience was . . .
   f. What my immediate impressions of you are.
   g. The ways in which we are similar or different are . . .

FRIENDSHIP RELATIONS EXERCISE

The following exercise is based upon the Johari Window. The objectives of the exercise are to examine your and the group's receptivity to feedback, willingness to self-disclose, and willingness to take risks in relations with friends.

The procedure for the exercise is as follows: Each person should complete the "Friendship Relations Survey." (The results should be recorded on the "Friendship Relations Survey Answer Sheet," p. 231.) Score the results by transferring the figures to the "Friendship Relations Survey Answer Key," p. 233. Follow the directions there and on the "Friendship Relations Survey Summary Sheet," p. 235, to get the final results of the survey for yourself and the group. (The group average is found by adding the scores of every member and dividing by the number of persons in the group.) Discuss the results in the group as a whole. The following questions may facilitate your discussion:

1. Share your thoughts and feelings about when it is appropriate to receive feedback from and to self-disclose with your friends.

2. Share your thoughts and feelings about when you want other members of the group to give feedback to you and when you will want to self-disclose to them.

3. Do you have a conservative or a risky group?

4. How does trust affect your receptivity to feedback and willingness to give feedback?

5. Would you like to change the way you are now behaving?

6. What would be productive and useful changes in your behavior in order to develop better relationships with your friends?

FRIENDSHIP RELATIONS SURVEY

This survey, which is based upon a managerial effectiveness survey developed by Jay Hall, is designed to assess your understanding of and behavior in your interpersonal relationships. There are no "right" or "wrong" answers. Rather, the *best* answer is simply the one which comes closest to representing your practices in your quest for *good interpersonal relationships.*

For each item on the survey you are requested to indicate which of the alternative reactions would be more characteristic of the way *you* would handle the situation described. Some alternatives may be equally characteristic of you or equally uncharacteristic. While this is a possibility, nevertheless choose the alternative which is *relatively* more characteristic of you. For each item, you will have five points that you may *distribute* in any of the following combinations:

	A	*B*
1. If *A* is completely characteristic of what you would do and *B* is completely uncharacteristic, write a "5" on your survey answer sheet under *A* and a "0" under *B*, thus:	5	0
2. If *A* is considerably characteristic of what you would do and *B* is somewhat characteristic, write a "4" on your survey answer sheet under *A* and a "1" under *B*, thus:	4	1
3. If *A* is only slightly more characteristic of what you would do than *B* is, write a "3" on your survey answer sheet under *A* and a "2" under *B*, thus:	3	2
4. Each of the above three combinations may be used in the converse order; that is, for example, should you feel *B* is slightly more characteristic of you than *A*, write a "2" on your survey answer sheet under *A* and a "3" under *B*, thus:	2	3

5. And so on for *A* = 1, *B* = 4; or *A* = 0, *B* = 5.

Thus there are six possible combinations for responding to the pair of alternatives presented to you with each survey item. *Be sure the numbers you assign to each pair sum to 5.* In general, try to relate each situation in the survey to your own personal experience. Take as much time as you need to make a true and accurate response. *There is no right or wrong answer.* Attempts to give a "correct" response merely distort the meaning of your answers and render the test results valueless. *Be honest with yourself!*

1. If a friend of mine had a "personality conflict" with a mutual acquaintance of ours with whom it was important for him to get along, I would:
   A. Tell my friend that I felt he was partially responsible for any problems with this other person and try to let him know how the person was being affected by him.
   B. Not get involved because I wouldn't be able to continue to get along with both of them once I had entered in in any way.

2. If one of my friends and I had had a heated argument in the past and I realized that he was ill at ease around me from that time on, I would:
   A. Avoid making things worse by discussing his behavior and just let the whole thing drop.
   B. Bring up his behavior and ask him how he felt the argument had affected our relationship.

3. If a friend began to avoid me and act in an aloof and withdrawn manner, I would:
   A. Tell him about his behavior and suggest that he tell me what was on his mind.
   B. Follow his lead and keep our contacts brief and aloof since that seems to be what he wants.

4. If two of my friends and I were talking and one of my friends slipped and brought up a personal problem of mine that involved the other friend, of which he was not yet aware, I would:
   A. Change the subject and signal my friend to do the same.
   B. Fill my uninformed friend in on what the other friend was talking about and suggest that we go into it later.

5. If a friend of mine were to tell me that, in his opinion, I was doing things that made me less effective than I might be in social situations, I would:
   A. Ask him to spell out or describe what he has observed and suggest changes I might make.
   B. Resent his criticism and let him know why I behave the way I do.

6. If one of my friends aspired to an office in our organization for which

I felt he was unqualified, and if he had been tentatively assigned to that position by the president of our group, I would:

A. Not mention my misgivings to either my friend or the president and let them handle it in their own way.

B. Tell my friend and the president of my misgivings and then leave the final decision up to them.

7. If I felt that one of my friends was being unfair to me and his other friends, but none of them had mentioned anything about it, I would:

A. Ask several of these people how they perceived the situation to see if they felt he was being unfair.

B. Not ask the others how they perceived our friend, but wait for them to bring it up with me.

8. If I were preoccupied with some personal matters and a friend told me that I had become irritated with him and others and that I was jumping on him for unimportant things, I would:

A. Tell him I was preoccupied and would probably be on edge for a while and would prefer not to be bothered.

B. Listen to his complaints but not try to explain my actions to him.

9. If I had heard some friends discussing an ugly rumor about a friend of mine which I knew could hurt him and he asked me what I knew about it, if anything, I would:

A. Say I didn't know anything about it and tell him no one would believe a rumor like that anyway.

B. Tell him exactly what I had heard, when I had heard it, and from whom I had heard it.

10. If a friend pointed out the fact that I had a personality conflict with another friend with whom it was important for me to get along, I would:

A. Consider his comments out of line and tell him I didn't want to discuss the matter any further.

B. Talk about it openly with him to find out how my behavior was being affected by this.

11. If my relationship with a friend has been damaged by repeated arguments on an issue of importance to us both, I would:

A. Be cautious in my conversations with him so the issue would not come up again to worsen our relationship.

B. Point to the problems the controversy was causing in our relationship and suggest that we discuss it until we get it resolved.

12. If in a personal discussion with a friend about his problems and behavior, he suddenly suggested we discuss my problems and behavior as well as his own, I would:

A. Try to keep the discussion away from me by suggesting that other, closer friends often talked to me about such matters.

B. Welcome the opportunity to hear what he felt about me and encourage his comments.

13. If a friend of mine began to tell me about his hostile feelings about another friend whom he felt was being unkind to others (and I agreed wholeheartedly), I would:
    A. Listen and also express my own feelings to him so he would know where I stood.
    B. Listen, but not express my own negative views and opinions because he might repeat what I said to him in confidence.

14. If I thought an ugly rumor was being spread about me and suspected that one of my friends had quite likely heard it, I would:
    A. Avoid mentioning the issue and leave it to him to tell me about it if he wanted to.
    B. Risk putting him on the spot by asking him directly what he knew about the whole thing.

15. If I had observed a friend in social situations and thought that he was doing a number of things which hurt his relationships, I would:
    A. Risk being seen as a busybody and tell him what I had observed and my reactions to it.
    B. Keep my opinions to myself rather than be seen as interfering in things that are none of my business.

16. If two friends and I were talking and one of them inadvertently mentioned a personal problem which involved me, but of which I knew nothing, I would:
    A. Press them for information about the problem and their opinions about it.
    B. Leave it up to my friends to tell me or not tell me, letting them change the subject if they wished.

17. If a friend seemed to be preoccupied and began to jump on me for seemingly unimportant things, and to become irritated with me and others without real cause, I would:
    A. Treat him with kid gloves for a while on the assumption that he was having some temporary personal problems which were none of my business.
    B. Try to talk to him about it and point out to him how his behavior was affecting people.

18. If I had begun to dislike certain habits of a friend to the point that it was interfering with my enjoying his company, I would:
    A. Say nothing to him directly, but let him know my feelings by ignoring him whenever his annoying habits were obvious.
    B. Get my feelings out in the open and clear the air so that we could continue our friendship comfortably and enjoyably.

19. In discussing social behavior with one of my more sensitive friends, I would:
    A. Avoid mentioning his flaws and weaknesses so as not to hurt his feelings.
    B. Focus on his flaws and weaknesses so he could improve his interpersonal skills.
20. If I knew I might be assigned to an important position in our group and my friends' attitudes towards me had become rather negative, I would:
    A. Discuss my shortcomings with my friends so I could see where to improve.
    B. Try to figure out my own shortcomings by myself so I could improve.

SELF-DISCLOSURE AND LIKING EXERCISE

The objective of this exercise is to examine the relationship between self-disclosure and liking for another person. The procedure is as follows:

1. Pair nonverbally with a person who is almost or entirely a stranger. No words are to be spoken. After two minutes of silence together privately, rate your liking for the other on the response form, p. 26.
2. During the next five minutes each person introduces himself to the other. You may say anything about yourself you think will help the other get to know you better. At the end of the five minutes the second rating is made by each person privately.
3. For five minutes communicate *nonverbally* with each other. You may touch the other's face, exchange hand clasps, walk arm-in-arm, dance, all without words. Then privately make the third rating of the other.
4. For five minutes tell the other your favorable first impressions of him. You may begin by saying, "The things I like most about you are . . ." Then privately make the fourth rating.
5. For the final five minutes tell your partner your *unfavorable* first impressions of him. You may begin by saying, "The things I don't like about you are . . ." Then privately make the fifth rating of the other.
6. Find the group average for each rating by adding all the individual scores and dividing by the number of individuals within the group.
7. Discuss the results.
   a. How did your liking for the other change from rating to rating?
   b. Was this similar to or different from the group averages?
   c. Usually the more two individuals self-disclose to each other the more they like each other. Was this true in your group?

d. What were your feelings during each of the experiences with your partner?

e. Was your partner honest with you? If not, would you have liked him better if he had been honest?

REACTION BALLOT: MY LIKING FOR MY PARTNER

Scale

10. Like better than any others I know
9. Like much
8. Like some
7. Like a little
6. Average or slightly better
5. Average or slightly below
4. Dislike a little
3. Dislike some
2. Dislike much
1. Dislike intensely; would prefer never to see again

RATINGS

Rate 1 to 10

First Rating:	Before speaking	_____
Second Rating:	After introductory conversation	_____
Third Rating:	After nonverbal communication	_____
Fourth Rating:	After sharing our first impressions of each other (Positive)	_____
Fifth Rating:	After sharing first impressions (Negative)	_____

SUMMARY TABLE

	Your Rating	*Group Average*
First Rating:	_____	_____
Second Rating:	_____	_____
Third Rating:	_____	_____
Fourth Rating:	_____	_____
Fifth Rating:	_____	_____

SELF-DESCRIPTION EXERCISE

The purpose of this exercise is to provide an interesting and enjoyable way to describe yourself to the other members of the group. For this exercise you need enough construction paper for each person to have three or four sheets; be sure to provide a variety of different colors. The procedure for the exercise is as follows:

1. Each person takes several sheets of construction paper. The color of the construction paper he takes should in some way describe what he is like or relate to his past experiences.

2. Each person builds something out of the construction paper which reflects what he is like. The shape of the object, the colors of the paper used, the kind of object built, all can reflect aspects of the person. One person may want to build a small bird made out of blue paper to describe himself; another person may want to build a red church; another might build a green bridge.

3. In the group as a whole, go around the circle and explain in what ways the construction reflects aspects of yourself. Other members may respond, ask questions, or provide feedback concerning the ways in which they perceive the person explaining his construction.

SELF-APPRAISAL EXERCISE

This activity is aimed at giving you a chance to look at the ways you relate to others. The form it uses was originally developed by Edgar Schein, Bernard Bass, and James Vaughan. On the basis of this form you may analyze the ways in which you may want to grow in order to develop more satisfying relationships with others. For each of the statements below, underline the number that best identifies your place on the scale. Next draw a diamond around the number which best expresses where you would like to be. (Example: 1 : 2 : <u>3</u> : 4 : ◇5◇ : 6 : 7 : 8 : 9)

1. *Ability to listen to others in an understanding way*
   Not at all   Completely
   able   1 : 2 : 3 : 4 : 5 : 6 : 7 : 8 : 9 able

2. *Willingness to discuss feelings with others*
   Completely   Completely
   unwilling   1 : 2 : 3 : 4 : 5 : 6 : 7 : 8 : 9 willing

3. *Awareness of the feelings of others*
Completely   Completely
unaware   1 : 2 : 3 : 4 : 5 : 6 : 7 : 8 : 9   aware

4. *Understanding why I do what I do*
No under-   Complete
standing   1 : 2 : 3 : 4 : 5 : 6 : 7 : 8 : 9   understanding

5. *Tolerance of conflict and antagonism*
Not tolerant   1 : 2 : 3 : 4 : 5 : 6 : 7 : 8 : 9   Tolerant

6. *Acceptance of expressions of affection and*
warmth among others
Uncom-
fortably   1 : 2 : 3 : 4 : 5 : 6 : 7 : 8 : 9   Readily

7. *Acceptance of comments about my behavior from others*
Rejecting   1 : 2 : 3 : 4 : 5 : 6 : 7 : 8 : 9   Welcoming

8. *Willingness to trust others*
Completely   Completely
suspicious   1 : 2 : 3 : 4 : 5 : 6 : 7 : 8 : 9   trusting

9. *Ability to influence others*
Completely   Completely
unable   1 : 2 : 3 : 4 : 5 : 6 : 7 : 8 : 9   able

10. *Relations with peers*
Wholly   Wholly
competitive   1 : 2 : 3 : 4 : 5 : 6 : 7 : 8 : 9   cooperative

After completing the form, sit down with two other persons and discuss the following:

1. Do they see your ways of relating to others the same way that you do?
2. What could you begin doing to change your style of relating to others so that it more nearly matches the way you would like to be?

ADJECTIVE CHECKLIST EXERCISE

The following exercise is aimed at providing an opportunity for the participants to disclose their view of themselves to the other members of their group and to receive feedback on how the other group members perceive them. The activities are as follows:

1. Each member should go through the list of adjectives and circle the six adjectives he thinks are most descriptive of himself.

2. Each member of the group then shares with the group the adjectives he circled. Members of the group then share with the person what adjectives they would have checked if they were to describe him. Do not spend more than five to ten minutes on each person in the group.

able	dutiful	irritable	passive
accepting	effervescent	jealous	paternal
adaptable	efficient	jovial	patient
aggressive	elusive	juvenile	perceptive
ambitious	energetic	kind	perfectionist
annoying	extroverted	knowledgeable	persuasive
anxious	fair	lazy	petty
authoritative	fearful	learned	playful
belligerent	foolish	lewd	pleasant
bitter	frank	liberal	pompous
bold	free	lively	powerful
brave	friendly	logical	pragmatic
calm	genial	loving	precise
carefree	gentle	malicious	pretending
careless	giving	manipulative	pretentious
caring	greedy	materialistic	principled
certain	gruff	maternal	progressive
cheerful	guilty	mature	protective
clever	gullible	merry	proud
cold	happy	modest	quarrelsome
complex	hard	mystical	questioning
confident	helpful	naive	quiet
conforming	helpless	narcissistic	radical
controlled	honorable	negative	rational
courageous	hostile	nervous	rationalizing
cranky	idealistic	neurotic	reactionary
critical	imaginative	noisy	realistic
cynical	immature	normal	reasonable
demanding	impressionable	·oblivious	reassuring
dependable	inconsiderate	objective	rebellious
dependent	independent	observant	reflective
derogatory	ingenious	obsessive	regretful
determined	innovative	organized	rejecting
dignified	insensitive	original	relaxed
disciplined	insincere	overburdened	reliable
docile	intelligent	overconfident	religious
dogged	introverted	overconforming	remote
domineering	intuitive	overemotional	resentful
dreamy	irresponsible	overprotecting	reserved

resolute	self-righteous	sympathetic	unpredictable
respectful	sensible	taciturn	unreasonable
responsible	sensitive	tactful	unstructured
responsive	sentimental	temperamental	useful
retentive	serious	tenacious	vain
rigid	shy	tender	vapid
sarcastic	silly	tense	visionary
satisfied	simple	thoughtful	vulnerable
scientific	sinful	tough	warm
searching	skillful	trusting	willful
self-accepting	sly	trustworthy	wise
self-actualizing	sociable	unassuming	wishful
self-assertive	spontaneous	unaware	withdrawn
self-aware	stable	uncertain	witty
self-conscious	strained	unconcerned	worried
self-effacing	strong	uncontrolled	youthful
self-indulgent	stubborn	understanding	zestful
selfish			

FANTASY EXERCISE

Self-disclosure is most clearly done when you tell others directly how you are reacting to the present situation. Yet many times we reveal ourselves in indirect ways, for example, by the jokes we tell, the things we find funny, the books we are interested in, or the movies we see. All these actions and attitudes tell other people something about ourselves. Often we may learn something about ourselves we were not fully aware of by analyzing our dreams, our daydreams, our interests, our values, or our humor. The following exercise lets you use your imagination in ways that may lead to a greater awareness of yourselves and which may help you get to know one another in a different and interesting way.

The following are a series of fantasy situations. They deal with initiating relationships with lonely people or giving help to individuals who seem to need it. The procedure for the exercise is as follows:

1. Divide into groups of three.
2. The leader presents an unfinished fantasy situation.
3. Each member of the triad thinks about his or her ending to the fantasy situation. If you want to, write out your ending.
4. In the triad each person shares his ending to the fantasy situation.
5. Each person should share with the other members of his triad what he has learned from the endings given to the fantasy situation about himself and about the other two members.

6. Switch partners and repeat steps 2, 3, 4, and 5. Do this for a series of situations, switching partners after each situation.

7. In the group as a whole, discuss what you have learned about yourself and the other members.

The fantasy situations are as follows:

1. You are walking down a dark street. Up ahead you see a streetlight. You walk nearer and nearer to the streetlight. Underneath the streetlight is a girl crying. What do you do? What happens?

2. You are eating lunch in a school cafeteria. You get your lunch and walk into the lunchroom. The lunchroom is crowded and noisy with lots of people laughing and shouting and having a good time. Off in a corner is a boy sitting all alone at a table. What do you do? What happens?

3. You are going to a party. You enter the party, take off your coat, find something to drink, and talk to a couple of friends. Standing all by himself in the middle of the room is a person you don't know. After ten minutes the person is still standing by himself. What do you do? What happens?

4. You are at a basketball game. It is half-time. You are talking with several of your friends. A person whom you casually met the week before is nearby. He is making obnoxious and embarrassing remarks to the people he is with. They all leave. You walk over to him and he insults you. What do you do? What happens?

5. You are sitting in class. Several persons in the class are making belittling comments towards another student. The student is obviously having his feelings hurt. He catches your eye and looks at you. What do you do? What happens?

6. You are watching a group of friends talking in front of a restaurant. A person whom they consider odd and strange walks up to them and tries to join in the conversation. They ignore him. Finally one of your friends says, "Why don't you get lost." The person turns away. What do you do? What happens?

7. You are sitting in a classroom. A student whom you don't know has constantly bugged the teacher and caused trouble ever since the class began several months ago. Although he is often funny, everyone is fed up with his behavior. He comes into the room and takes a seat next to you. What do you do? What happens?

8. There is a new student in the school. You have often heard her say that your school is not nearly as good as the school she previously attended and that the students at your school are really "just unreal"

and "really think they're cool" while she praises the students at her previous school. You meet her walking out of the school door. What do you do? What happens?

BAG EXERCISE

This exercise is to be used in connection with the presentation of the Johari Window. The exercise focuses on the thinking through of the things about yourself that you commonly share with other individuals (that is, your free areas) and the things that you do not commonly share with other individuals (that is, your hidden areas). In addition, it opens up the opportunity for each person to receive feedback from the other group members concerning how they see him. The materials needed for the exercise are as follows:

1. A ten-pound paper bag for each person.
2. One or two popular magazines such as *Life* for each person.
3. Construction paper of several different colors.
4. Yarn, string, and some small toys or any other objects that will help in constructing the bags.
5. Crayons, paints, or pencils for drawing.
6. Tape, paste or glue.

The procedure for the exercise is as follows:

1. Each person in the group gets a paper bag. Various materials described above are scattered around the room.
2. Each person spends half an hour building his bag. On the outside of the bag you should attach things that represent aspects of yourself that you commonly share with other people. On the inside of the bag you should place things that represent aspects of yourself that you do not commonly share with others. You may cut pictures, words, phrases, or slogans out of the magazines, draw designs or pictures, make objects out of the construction paper, or use anything else which seems relevant to illustrate the free and hidden aspects of yourself.
3. After everyone has finished, a group meeting is begun in which anyone may volunteer to talk about his bag. You may want to talk just about the outside of the bag, or you may feel like sharing part or all of what you have inside your bag. Everyone should feel free to share as much or as little as he would like to. You may want to keep working on your bag for a few days, adding things to the outside and inside, and then share it with the group at a later date.

4. After a person has shared part or all of his bag, the other members of the group may wish to comment on how their perceptions of the person match what they have heard. You may feel that the person left out qualities that you appreciate in him or perceive him as having. You may be surprised by finding that something the person felt was in his free area you have never seen in his behavior. Whatever your impressions of the person and your reactions to his bag, you should feel free to share them with him, using the characteristics of good feedback.

5. So that everyone who wants to may share his bag, you may want to put a time limit on how long the group may focus upon one person. Try to ensure that everyone who wants to share part or all of his bag has the opportunity to do so within the time limit set for the session.

FEEDBACK EXERCISES

Many of the exercises described in this chapter involve giving and receiving feedback. Feedback from others is the primary means by which you can increase your self-awareness. Since your ability to self-disclose depends upon your awareness of what you are like, it is important for you to receive as much feedback as possible from others on their impressions of you and how they are reacting to your behavior in the group. If not much feedback has been given and received during the other exercises, the group may wish to spend some time sharing their impressions of and reactions to each other. This can be done simply by stating, "My impression of you is . . . ," or "My reactions to your behavior are . . . ," or "The way I feel about you is . . . ." Be sure to observe the rules for constructive feedback.

Sometimes you may be unsure of what your impressions are of another person or of how you are reacting to his behavior. One way to clarify your impressions of and reactions to a person is to associate some animal, bird, song, color, weather, movie, book, food, or fantasy with the person. You may want to ask yourself, "What animal do I associate with this person: a puppy, a fox, a rabbit?" Or you may wish to ask yourself, "What books do I associate with this person; what songs do I associate with this person?" Finally, you may wish to ask yourself, "What fantasies do I associate with this person? Is he a knight in shining armor, an innkeeper in medieval England, a French chef, a conforming business executive, a professional singer?" Through stating to that person what animal, song, color, weather, movie, food, book, or fantasy you associate with him you may clarify your impressions and reactions and provide him with some interesting, entertaining, and helpful feedback.

INTERPERSONAL PATTERNS EXERCISE

The following exercise focuses upon your interaction with other individuals. It may help you think about how you behave when you initiate a relationship with another person or how you act in a group. The procedure for the exercise is as follows:

1. Divide into groups of three. Each person fills out the adjective check list.
2. Analyze the meaning of the adjectives you checked by following the instructions which are found following the check list.
3. Share with the other two members of your triad the results of the exercise and ask for their comments on whether they perceive you similarly or differently than the results of this exercise indicate.

The 20 verbs listed below describe some of the ways people feel and act from time to time. Think of your behavior in interaction with other people. How do you feel and act with other people? Check the five verbs which best describe your behavior in interaction with others as you see it.

_____ acquiesces	_____ disapproves
_____ advises	_____ evades
_____ agrees	_____ initiates
_____ analyzes	_____ judges
_____ assists	_____ leads
_____ concedes	_____ obliges
_____ cooperates	_____ relinquishes
_____ coordinates	_____ resists
_____ criticizes	_____ retreats
_____ directs	_____ withdraws

There are two underlying factors or traits involved in the list of adjectives: _dominance_ (authority or control) and _sociability_ (intimacy or friendliness). Most people tend to like to control things (high dominance) or to let others control things (low dominance). Similarly most people tend to be very warm and personal (high sociability) or to be somewhat cold and impersonal (low sociability). In the following boxes circle the 5 adjectives you used to describe yourself in group activity. The set in which 3 or more adjectives are circled out of the 5 represents your interpersonal pattern tendency in that group.

	High Dominance	Low Dominance
High Sociability	advises coordinates directs initiates leads	acquiesces agrees assists cooperates obliges
Low Sociability	analyzes criticizes disapproves judges resists	concedes evades relinquishes retreats withdraws

EXERCISE IN SELF-DISCLOSURE

This exercise is based upon an exercise created by F. R. Fosmire and J. L. Wallen. It involves discussing different aspects of self-disclosure to other individuals. The objective of this exercise is to help you think about the area of interpersonal openness in a systematic way. In your group discuss for the next 20 minutes the following questions:

1. What are the risks in being self-disclosing with another person? When is it better not to be open about your reactions to another person? Give examples.

2. What are the benefits from being self-disclosing with another person? When is it necessary and when is it merely helpful? Give examples.

3. Does self-disclosure refer only to verbal behavior? Can a person be self-disclosing without using words?

4. What kinds of behavior can lead you to feel that you are being self-disclosing when others do not see you as self-disclosing at all?

5. Is there a difference between "telling somebody off" and being self-disclosing with him? Is there a difference between passing judgment on another person and being self-disclosing with him?

The next phase of this exercise focuses upon the kinds of behavior that indicate that you are ready for others to share with you their reactions to your behavior and their impressions of you. In your group discuss the following questions:

1. What do the members of your group do that leads you to feel that they want or do not want you to be self-disclosing with them?
2. Describe specific actions of any member that (1) make it easier to be self-disclosing with him or (2) make it difficult for you to be self-disclosing with him.
3. Take no more than 20 minutes to share these impressions with your fellow group members. Then see if the group can draw some general conclusions about what helps and what hinders self-disclosure in others.

The next part of the exercise focuses on constructive self-disclosure. It is based on the assumption that we may self-disclose in ways that enhance a relationship or in ways that threaten it.

1. Each person should name the group members whose self-disclosure he finds most comfortable. That is, name the group members with whom you would be most comfortable about having share their honest reactions to something you have said or done with the group.
2. What do these group members do that leads you to be receptive to their self-disclosure about their reactions to your behavior? What do other group members do that results in your being less receptive to their being self-disclosing with you?
3. Take no more than 30 minutes to share these impressions with your group members. Then try to draw some conclusions about what helps and what hinders receptiveness in others.
4. Read and discuss the next section, entitled "Constructive Self-Disclosure."

CONSTRUCTIVE SELF-DISCLOSURE [2]

People rarely talk openly about their reactions to each other's behavior. Most of us withhold our feelings about the other person (even in relations that are very important or dear to us) because we are afraid of hurting the other person, making him angry, or being rejected by him. Because we do not know how to be constructively self-disclosing, we say

2 The material in this section was originally developed by J. L. Wallen.

nothing. The other person continues to be totally unaware of our re-action to his actions. Likewise we continue to be ignorant of the effect our actions produce in him. Consequently, many relations that could be productive and enjoyable gradually deteriorate under the accumulated load of tiny annoyances, hurt feelings, and misunderstandings that were never talked about openly.

The following points increase the chances that self-disclosure will im-prove a relationship rather than harm it.

1. Self-disclosure must begin with a *desire to improve your relationship with the other person.* Self-disclosure is not an end in itself but a means to an end. We are not open with people when we do not care about them. When you are trying to establish an open sharing of reactions with another person, try to let him know that this means you value your relationship with him and wish to improve it *be-cause* it is important.

2. Try to create a shared understanding of your relationship. You wish to know how the other person perceives and feels about your actions. You want him to know how you perceive and feel about his actions. Each of you will then view the relationship from more nearly the same viewpoint.

3. Realize that self-disclosure involves *risk-taking.* Your willingness to risk being rejected or hurt by the other person depends on how im-portant the relationship is to you. You cannot tell that the other person will not become angry or feel hurt by what you say. The im-portant point is that you are willing to risk his being himself, what-ever he feels, in the effort to make the encounter into a learning situa-tion for both of you.

4. Although the discussion may become intense, spirited, angry, or tear-ful, it should be *noncoercive* and should not be an attempt to make the other person change. Each person 'should use the information as he sees fit. The attitude should not be "Who's wrong and who's right?" but "What can each of us learn from this discussion that will make our relationship more productive and more satisfying?" As a result of the discussion one, both, or neither of you may act differently in the future. Each of you, however, will act with fuller awareness of the effect of his actions on the other as well as with more understanding of the other person's intentions. Any change will thus be self-chosen rather than compelled by a desire to please or to submit to the other.

5. Timing is important. Reactions should be shared at a time as close to the behavior that aroused them as possible so that both persons will know exactly what behavior is being discussed. For example,

you can comment on behavior during the encounter itself: "What you just said is the kind of remark that makes me feel pushed away."

6. Disturbing situations should be discussed as they happen; hurt feelings and annoyances should not be saved up and dropped on another person all at one time.

7. Paraphrase the other person's comments about you to make sure you understand them as he means them. Check to make sure the other understands your comments in the way you mean them.

8. Statements are more helpful if they are
Specific rather than general: "You bumped my plate," rather than "You never watch where you're going."
Tentative rather than absolute: "You seem unconcerned about Jimmy," rather than "You don't give a damn about Jimmy and never will."
Informing rather than ordering: "I hadn't finished yet," rather than "Stop interrupting me."

9. Use perception-checking responses to insure that you are not making false assumptions about the other's feelings. "I thought you weren't interested in trying to understand my idea. Was I wrong?" "Did my last statement bother you?"

10. The least helpful kinds of statements are those that sound as if they are information about the other person but are really expressions of your own feelings. Avoid the following:
Judgments about the other: "You never pay any attention."
Name-calling, trait labeling: "You're a phony"; "You're too rude."
Accusations; imputing undesirable motives to the other: "You enjoy putting people down"; "You always have to be the center of attention."
Commands and orders: "Stop laughing"; "Don't talk so much."
Sarcasm: "You always look on the bright side of things, don't you?" (when the opposite is meant).

11. The most helpful kinds of information about yourself and your reactions are
Behavior descriptions. To develop skills in describing another person's behavior you must sharpen your skills in observing what actually did occur. Let others know what behavior you are responding to by describing it clearly and specifically enough that they know what you saw. To do this you must describe visible evidence, behavior that is open to anybody's observation. Restrict yourself to talking about the things the other person did.

Examples: "Bob, you seem to disagree with whatever Harry suggests today." (*Not* "Bob, you're just trying to show Harry up."

This is not a description but an accusation of unworthy motives.)

"Jim, you've talked more than others on this topic. Several times you interrupted others before they had finished." (*Not* "Jim, you're too rude!" which names a trait and gives no evidence. *Not* "Jim, you always want to hog the center of attention" which imputes an unworthy motive or intention.)

"Sam, I had not finished my statement when you interrupted me." (*Not* "Sam, you deliberately didn't let me finish." The word *deliberately* implies that Sam knowingly and intentionally cut you off. All anybody can observe is that he did interrupt you.)

Descriptions of your own feelings. You should attempt to describe your feelings about the other person's actions so that your feelings are seen as temporary and capable of change rather than as permanent. It is better to say, "At this point I'm very annoyed with you," than "I dislike you and I always will."

You may see how well you understand this section by indicating which of the following statements are good guidelines for self-disclosure that is meant to improve a relationship. (Answers are on p. 41.)

1. Self-disclosure should try to make the other person improve his behavior.
2. Self-disclosure should be a two-way street, a shared understanding.
3. Self-disclosure involves risk-taking.
4. Statements are more helpful if they are tentative, specific, and informing.
5. Wait to discuss disturbing situations after several have built up.
6. The most helpful kinds of information about your reactions are descriptions of the other person's behavior that you are responding to and descriptions of your own feelings.
7. The most helpful kinds of information about yourself are details of your past life.

Indicate which of the following are helpful self-disclosures (answers on p. 41):

1. John tells Mary to leave him alone.
2. Mary tells John that at this moment she feels hurt and rejected by his behavior.

3. Sandy tells Jane that Jane is domineering.

4. Bill says to Sam, "You look angry. Are you?"

5. Dave says to Brenda, "Are you saying that I have been ignoring you the past two weeks?"

SELF-DESCRIPTION

Who am I? What am I like? How do others perceive me? What are my strengths as a person? What areas do I want to develop greater skills in? At this point you have participated in a series of exercises aimed at increasing your self-awareness and your skills in self-disclosing. You should now sit down and try to summarize what you have learned about yourself. In the following space, write a description of what you are like. Use the five questions stated above for a guide.

_____

_____

_____

_____

_____

_____

_____

_____

_____

_____

_____

_____

_____

_____

_____

_____

_____

_____

_____

_____

_____

_____

_____

CHECKLIST OF SKILLS

In this chapter we have focused upon being self-disclosing, increasing self-awareness, and giving and receiving feedback. Rate yourself on your level of skills for each of the following:

1. *My ability to be appropriately self-disclosing is*
   Terrible 1 : 2 : 3 : 4 : 5 : 6 : 7 : 8 : 9 Excellent
2. *My ability to give constructive feedback is*
   Terrible 1 : 2 : 3 : 4 : 5 : 6 : 7 : 8 : 9 Excellent
3. *My willingness to receive feedback is*
   Terrible 1 : 2 : 3 : 4 : 5 : 6 : 7 : 8 : 9 Excellent
4. *My level of self-awareness is*
   Very low 1 : 2 : 3 : 4 : 5 : 6 : 7 : 8 : 9 Very high
5. I need more work on the following:

   _____ Self-disclosure.

   _____ Giving constructive feedback.

   _____ Being willing to receive feedback.

   _____ Increasing my self-awareness.

ANSWERS

Page 12: 1: true; 2: true; 3: false; 4: false; 5: false; 6: false; 7: true; 8: true; 9: false

Page 15: 1: a. hidden, b. blind, c. free, d. unknown; 2: b

Pages 17–18: 1: b; 2: a. false, b. false, c. true, d. true, e. false, f. true, g. false

Page 39: 2, 3, 4, 6

Pages 39–40: 2, 4, 5

The Development and Maintenance of Trust

In Chapter 2 it was emphasized that, to develop a relationship with another person, you must disclose yourself in order to let him get to know you. Engaging in self-disclosure involves being self-aware and self-accepting. In addition, self-disclosure frequently involves the risk of rejection and ridicule. To self-disclose in a meaningful way, you must trust the other person will not respond in a way which will hurt your feelings or make you feel rejected. Thus a third element in the use of self-disclosure is your willingness to risk being rejected in order to build a close relationship. At this point, trust between two individuals in a relationship becomes of central importance.

CLIMATE OF TRUST

Little happens in a relationship until the individuals learn to trust each other. Because of this, forming a climate of trust is one of the most important tasks. In fact, the first crisis most relationships face involve the ability of two individuals to trust themselves and each other. Trust is absolutely essential for a relationship to grow and develop. In order to facilitate the development of a relationship, you must learn to create a climate of trust which reduces your own and the other person's fears of betrayal and rejection and builds the hopes of acceptance and support. Creating a climate of trust involves self-disclosure on the part of everyone involved. A person who dares to entrust himself to others goes far in creating a climate of trust in a relationship.

In studying this chapter the reader should seek (1) to arrive at an understanding of what trust is and what it is not, (2) to understand how trust is developed in a relationship, (3) to experience a situation in which trust is either developed or destroyed, and (4) to arrive at a summary conclusion about the role of trust in relationships.

DEFINITION OF TRUST

What is it like to trust another person? When are you being trusting and when are you not? When are you behaving in a trustworthy way and when are you violating someone else's trust? How do you recognize trust when you see it? Trust is a word everyone uses, yet it is a very complex concept and difficult to define. Based upon the writings of Deutsch (1962) and others, trust may be defined as including the following elements:

1. You are in a situation where a choice to trust another person can lead to either beneficial or harmful consequences for your needs and goals. Thus you realize there is a risk involved in trusting.
2. You realize that whether the consequences are beneficial or harmful depends upon the future behavior of another person.
3. You expect to suffer more if the consequences are harmful than you will gain if they are beneficial.
4. You feel relatively confident that the other person will behave in such a way that the beneficial consequences will result.

Thus the mother who leaves her child with a baby-sitter makes a trusting choice because the mother presumably (1) is aware that her choice could lead to harmful or beneficial consequences, (2) realizes that the consequences of her choice depend upon the behavior of the baby-sitter, (3) would expect to suffer much more if her trust in the baby-sitter were violated (and her child were harmed) than she would gain if her trust were fulfilled (she is free to do her shopping), and (4) feels relatively confident that the baby-sitter will behave in such a way that the consequences will be beneficial.

BUILDING INTERPERSONAL TRUST

In developing a relationship, you establish trust in a commitment period in which two individuals disclose more and more of themselves and their reactions to the immediate situation and each other. As was discussed in the previous chapter, a relationship is built as two individuals get to know and understand each other better. Getting to know one another depends upon both persons being self-disclosing. The potential gain from being self-disclosing is building a closer relationship; the potential loss is being rejected or being held in disrespect or contempt. It is by your willingness to risk rejection by self-disclosing in order to build a closer relationship that your trust is established and the relationship grows and develops. When you disclose to another person, trust is built if he responds to you with acceptance and support. This leads to a growing confidence that the other will not purposely hurt you. Trust is destroyed, however, if he responds to you with rejection or ridicule. This leads you to feel that the other person will purposely hurt you. Thus there are two basic elements to building trust in a relationship. The first involves one person taking risks by self-disclosure, and the second involves the other responding with acceptance and support.

According to our definition of trust, when you self-disclose to another person you are engaging in trust when you

1. are aware that your choice to be open could lead to beneficial (a closer relationship) or harmful (rejection, ridicule) consequences;
2. realize that the consequences of your choice depend upon the behavior of the other person;
3. expect to suffer much more if your trust is violated (and you are rejected) than you would gain if your trust is fulfilled (and the relationship develops);
4. feel relatively confident that the other will behave in such a way that the beneficial consequences will result.

Not all self-disclosure may involve trust, but the type of self-disclosure which really moves a relationship forward will involve trust.

Chapter 2 of this book dealt with self-disclosure. In this chapter, therefore, we will not discuss the first element of building trust, namely, taking risks in disclosing yourself to another person. Just remember not to reveal yourself so fast to another person that he is overpowered and bewildered. This chapter discusses your responding to the other person's risk-taking in his self-disclosure.

You may test your understanding of the previous sections by answering the following questions (answers on p. 59):

1. Which of the following are involved in a situation of trust?
   a. A risk which can lead to either beneficial or harmful consequences.
   b. Whether beneficial or harmful consequences result depends upon your behavior.

c. You will gain more from the beneficial consequences than you will suffer by the harmful consequences.

d. You are relatively confident that the other person will be helpful.

2. What are the two basic elements of building trust in a relationship?
   a. One person tells off his boss.
   b. The first person takes risks with self-disclosure.
   c. The second person is noncommital and nonjudgmental.
   d. The second person is accepting and supportive.

3. Which of the following are examples of trusting behavior?
   a. Playing poker.
   b. A shy person asking a girl he doesn't know very well for a date.
   c. Telling a friend he has bad breath.
   d. Avoiding people.
   e. Deepening your level of self-disclosure with a friend.

RESPONDING TO OTHER PERSON'S RISKS IN A TRUSTWORTHY WAY

Probably the first and deepest concern to arise in a relationship is acceptance. Two points concerning acceptance need to be made. The first is that acceptance of others usually results from and begins with acceptance of yourself. This was discussed in Chapter 2. The second is that acceptance is the key to reducing your anxiety and fears about being vulnerable. Defensive feelings of fear and distrust are common blocks to the functioning of a person and to the development of constructive relationships. This means that one of the first things to do in building a friendship is to create a relationship that continues to reduce the fears and distrust of yourself and the other person. Trust is built by accepting the other and keeping the communication as open, helpful, and complete as possible. If the person risking self-disclosure does not feel accepted, he will not trust you and will not engage in further self-disclosure in the future.

In a trusting situation, the person initiating trust is dependent upon the other person not to take advantage of his vulnerability. Vulnerability exists when a person has taken a risk that exposes him to harmful consequences such as rejection or ridicule. Because of the initiator's vulnerability, the receiver temporarily has power over the initiator's feelings. He can make the initiator feel good by being accepting and supporting, or he can make him feel bad by being rejecting and ridiculing. The receiver builds trust when he does not take advantage of the initiator's vulnerability. When the receiver uses his power to harm the initiator, he destroys trust. Being trustworthy means using your power to build the relationship, not to take advantage of the other person's vulnerability.

More specifically, in a relationship where the other person has taken a risk in self-disclosure, you are trustworthy to the extent that you

1. Express acceptance and support for the person (but not always for his behavior).
2. Reciprocate with appropriate self-disclosure.

The Key to Building Trust in a Relationship is Being Trustworthy. In a later chapter we will discuss in depth the ways in which acceptance and support are communicated. At this point, however, the point should be made that the expression of warmth towards the other person in a relationship builds a high level of interpersonal trust because it increases the other person's expectations that you will respond with acceptance and support when he self-discloses. In addition, the congruence of your verbal statements, nonverbal cues such as facial expression and tone of voice, and your behavior will affect the other person's perception of your trustworthiness. If you are frowning while you say you like the other person and you then walk away, your statement will not be seen as being very trustworthy.

The implications of this discussion about developing trust are that there are primarily two types of behavior that will decrease trust in a relationship. The first involves the nonreciprocation of self-disclosure. To the extent that you are closed and the other person is open, he will not trust you. If someone discloses himself and you do not reciprocate, he will often feel overexposed and very vulnerable. The second behavior is rejection, ridicule, or disrespect as a response to the other person's self-disclosure. Making a joke at the expense of another person, laughing at the person's self-disclosure, moralizing about the other person, or being evaluative in your response, all communicate rejection. This will effectively silence the other person and destroy some of the trust in the relationship.

TRUSTING AS A SELF-FULFILLING PROPHECY

Consider the case of two individuals who join a new group. One expects the group members to dislike and reject him and, therefore, he is very guarded and suspicious of the other group members. This behavior makes them withdraw and look elsewhere for a friendly companion. "See," he might say, "I was right. I knew they would reject me." The other new member, however, comes to the group expecting that almost everyone will be congenial, friendly, and trustworthy; he initiates warmth and friendliness, and consequently he finds his fellow group members to be all that he expected. Each of these individuals has made a self-fulfilling prophecy.

A self-fulfilling prophecy is, in the beginning, a false definition of a situation that evokes a new behavior, one which makes it possible for the originally false impression to come true. The assumptions you make about other people and the way in which you then behave often influence how other people respond, thus creating self-fulfilling prophecies in interpersonal relationships. We usually conform to the expectations others have for us. If we feel that they do not trust us and expect us to violate their trust, we will often do so. If we feel that they trust us and expect us to be trustworthy, we will often be that way. In building trust in a relationship the expectations you have about the other person may influence how you act toward him, thus setting up the possibility of a self-fulfilling prophecy. There is a lot to be said for assuming that other people are trustworthy.

You may assess your understanding of the above sections by answering the following questions (answers on p. 59):

1. What are the two most important points made about acceptance?
   a. If you accept others, they will accept you.
   b. In order to accept another person, you must interact with him.
   c. Acceptance is the key to reducing fears and anxieties about vulnerability.
   d. Acceptance of other people usually begins with acceptance of yourself.

2. What is a self-fulfilling prophecy?
   a. A true definition of a situation that brings out old behavior and makes it possible for the originally true definition to be false.
   b. A prophecy made by an old Tibetan monk after he has discovered who he is.
   c. A false definition of a situation that brings out new behavior that makes it possible for the originally false definition to come true.

3. Which of the following are responses that will help build trust after the other person has taken a risk in self-disclosing his feelings about the situation you are both in?
   a. Expressing warmth towards him.
   b. Walking away without saying a word.
   c. Telling him your feelings about the situation.
   d. Expressing acceptance and support.
   e. Laughing at his feelings.
   f. Making a joke out of his self-disclosure.
   g. Changing the subject.
   h. Saying, "I'm very interested to hear that" in a bored, uninterested way.
   i. Telling him whether his feelings are right or wrong.
   j. Checking to make sure you understand his feelings while you express interest and warmth.

PRISONER'S DILEMMA GAME

The game you are about to play is called the prisoner's dilemma game. It is a game in which a player has to choose between increasing his own immediate gain or increasing the total gain of both players. It derives its name from the following situation (Luce & Raiffa, 1957):

> Two suspects are taken into custody and separated. The District Attorney is certain that they are guilty of a specific crime, but he does not have adequate evidence to convict them at a trial. He points out each prisoner's alternatives to him: to confess to the crime that the police are sure they have committed, or not to confess. If they both do not confess, then the District Attorney states he will book them on some very minor but trumped-up charge such as petty larceny and illegal possession of a weapon for which they would both receive minor punishments; if they both confess they will be prosecuted, but he will recommend less than the most severe sentence; but if one confesses and the other does not, then the confessor will receive lenient treatment for turning state's evidence, whereas the latter will get "the book" slapped at him (p. 95).

Neither prisoner is aware of the other prisoner's decision. The decision of each will be very much affected by his prediction of what the other prisoner will do. Both decisions will be very much affected by the extent to which each trusts the other not to confess. The important properties of this dilemma appear in the "Prisoner's Dilemma Matrix."

PRISONER'S DILEMMA MATRIX

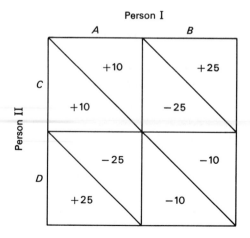

In the matrix it is clear that the number of points a person receives from a choice depends not only upon his own choice but upon what the choice of the other person is. If Person I chooses A, how many points he receives depends upon whether Person II chooses C or D. If Person I chooses A, and Person II chooses C, each will receive 10 points. If Person I chooses A, and Person II chooses D, Person I will lose 25 points and Person II will gain 25 points. If Person I chooses B, and Person II chooses C, Person I will gain 25 points and Person II will lose 25 points. And if Person I chooses B and Person II chooses D, both will lose 10 points. Study this matrix until you are sure you understand it. Then answer the following questions (answers on p. 59):

1. If Person II chooses C and Person I chooses A, Person I receives _____ points and Person II receives _____ points.

2. If Person II chooses C and Person I chooses B, Person I receives _____ points and Person II receives _____ points.

3. If Person II chooses D and Person I chooses A, Person I receives _____ points and Person II receives _____ points.

4. If Person II chooses D and Person I chooses B, Person I receives _____ points and Person II receives _____ points.

When you understand the matrix, you are ready to play the prisoner's dilemma game. The objective of the game is to provide an experience in which trust is either built and maintained or violated and diminished. To play the game each person needs a small pad of paper and a pencil. The procedure for the game is as follows:

1. Pair up with another person in the group. Sit back-to-back so that you cannot see the other player. Each person should have a pencil and a small pad of paper. One person is designated as Person I and the other as Person II.

2. When the leader gives the signal, each person should make his choice (Person I chooses between A and B, Person II chooses between C and D). Next, when the leader gives the signal, each person passes a slip of paper with his choice written on it over his shoulder to the other player. You may not speak; no communication to the other player other than the choice you make is allowed.

3. This is repeated 10 times. Each player should keep track of the number of points he has on the record sheet, p. 237.

4. At the end of the 10th choice, the two players can discuss anything they want to with each other for 10 minutes.

5. Ten more choices are made, following the procedure outlined in Step 2.

6. At the end of the 20th choice, total your gains and losses. Then fill out the questionnaire found under the heading "Impressions of Other's Behavior" (p. 52).

7. In the group as a whole, discuss the following questions:
   a. What were your feelings and reactions about yourself and the other player during the game?
   b. How many points did you make during the game? How many did the other player make?
   c. How did you describe the other player's behavior during the game? How did he describe your behavior during the game?
   d. Did the two of you trust each other? Were the two of you trustworthy?
   e. How did it feel to have your trust violated (if this happened to you)? How did it feel to violate the other player's trust?
   f. How was trust built during the game (if it was)?
   g. What impact did the period of communication have upon the way you played the game? Did it affect the way you felt about the other player's behavior?

The essential psychological feature of the prisoner's dilemma game is that there is no possibility for "rational" individual behavior in it unless the conditions for mutual trust exist. If each player chooses B and D to obtain either maximum gain or minimum loss for himself, each will lose. But it makes no sense to choose the other alternative, A and C, which could result in maximum loss, unless you can trust the other player. If you have to play the game, you either develop mutual trust or resign yourself to a loss by choosing competitively (that is, choosing B and D) in order to minimize your loss.

There has been a great deal of research on trust using the prisoner's dilemma game. Some of the conclusions from that research are as follows:

1. Trust is very often very hard to build but very easy to destroy. It may take two players a long time to arrive at a point where both consistently choose A and C, and any deviation to B or D may destroy all possibility of a cooperative solution to the dilemma.

2. Inappropriate trust may be just as dysfunctional as no trust at all; when a person consistently makes a trusting choice (A or C) and the other player consistently chooses B or D, the player exploiting the first person's trust will often feel little or no guilt by assuming that anyone who keeps making himself vulnerable deserves to be taken advantage of.

3. How the situation is defined will affect how easily trust may be built. If the game is defined as a problem-solving situation that the two

individuals must solve, trust is relatively easy to build. If the game is defined as a competitive situation in which you must win more points than the other player, trust is very difficult to build.

Thus in a situation in which you are attempting to increase trust, you may want to avoid violating the other person's trust, avoid trusting the other person if he consistently behaves in untrustworthy ways, and ensure that the situation is defined as a problem-solving situation, not a competitive one.

IMPRESSIONS OF OTHER'S BEHAVIOR

Indicate, by checking the appropriate spaces in the table following, your impression of the other player's behavior during the game. You may know the other player; if so, ignore everything you have felt about the person in the past and rate *only* your impressions of his behavior during the game.

_____warm	_____cold
_____trustworthy	_____untrustworthy
_____fair	_____unfair
_____generous	_____selfish
_____congenial	_____uncongenial
_____cooperative	_____competitive
_____kind	_____unkind
_____trustful	_____untrustful

DISCLOSURES CONCERNING TRUST LEVELS

The purpose of this exercise is for members of the group to disclose to one another their perceptions of the depth of the trust level in their relationship. Once this information is out in the open, the members of the group can discuss how trust could be increased in their relationship. Openly discussing issues concerning one's relationships is perhaps the most effective way to increase the closeness of the relationship. The procedure for the exercise is as follows:

1. Pick the individual whom you trust least in the group and pair off with him.

2. For 15 minutes, both individuals share their perceptions of why the trust level is low in their relationship. Try to avoid being defensive or hostile. Try to understand as fully as possible why the other person feels the way he does.

3. For the next 10 minutes, both individuals share their impressions of how the trust level in the relationship can be increased. This may involve stating how you are going to behave differently or how you would like the other to behave differently. Be as specific as possible.

4. Answer the following questions with your partner:
   a. To what extent is the lack of self-disclosure by one or both persons contributing to the relatively low level of trust in the relationship?
   b. To what extent is the lack of communicated support and acceptance by one or both persons contributing to the relatively low level of trust in the relationship?

5. Now find the person in the group whom you trust the most. Pair up with him.

6. For 15 minutes, both individuals share their understanding of why the trust level is high in their relationship. Try to understand as fully as possible why each person feels the way he does.

7. For 10 minutes, both individuals share their impressions of how the trust level in the relationship can be increased even higher. This may involve stating how you are going to behave differently or how you would like the other to behave differently. Be as specific as possible.

8. Answer the following questions with your partner:
   a. To what extent is the level of self-disclosure by one or both persons contributing to the relatively high level of trust in the relationship?
   b. To what extent is the communication of acceptance and support by one or both persons contributing to the relatively high level of trust in the relationship?

In this exercise it is possible to focus upon two important aspects of building and maintaining trust in a relationship. The first is the risk in self-disclosure you and your partners took. The second is the response you and your partners made to the other person's risk-taking. Both the risks and the responses are crucial elements of building trust in a relationship.

How do you self-disclose about your perceptions of and your feelings about your relationship with another person in ways which will result in a closer relationship? This question will be answered in depth in the next chapter, which focuses upon communication. But if your self-disclosures include the following four elements, you have a good chance of successfully moving the relationship closer:

1. *Statement of your intentions:* For example, "I'm worried about our relationship. I want to do something which will help us become better friends."

2. *Statement of your expectations about how the other person may respond:* For example, "I think you may be uncomfortable about my bringing this up but that you will listen and try to understand what I am saying."

3. *Statement of what you will do if he violates your expectations:* For example, "If you shut me off, I will be hurt and will become defensive."

4. *Statement of how trust will be reestablished if he violates your expectations and you make your response:* For example, "If you cut me off and I become defensive, then we'll have to spend an evening talking about old times to get ourselves back together again."

To the extent that these four points become clear in the conversation in which you take a risk, you may feel more confident that the relationship will not be damaged even if the risk turns out badly.

The response you make to another person's risk-taking is crucial for building trust in the relationship. The other person will feel it is safe to take risks in self-disclosure to the extent that he feels he will receive support when necessary and acceptance rather than rejection. To ensure that the relationship grows you should:

1. Make sure the other person feels supported for taking the risk.

2. If you disagree with what he is saying, make sure that it is clear that it is his ideas you are rejecting, not him as a person.

3. Make sure you disclose your perceptions and feelings about the relationship. Always reward openness with openness when you are dealing with friends or individuals with whom you wish to develop a closer relationship.

Answer the following questions (answers on p. 59):

1. What four elements should you have in a conversation when you are taking a risk in self-disclosure in a relationship?
   a. An initial statement of neutral interest.
   b. A statement of your intentions.
   c. A statement of your expectations about how the other person may respond.
   d. A comment on the weather.
   e. A statement of what you will do if the other person violates your expectation.

f. A statement of how the other person bothers you.

g. A statement of how trust will be reestablished.

2. When the other person takes a risk in self-disclosure, what three things should you work into the conversation?

a. Make sure the other person feels supported for taking the risk.

b. Make sure you do not reveal your feelings about the situation.

c. Make sure you never show lack of interest.

d. Make sure, if you disagree, that the other person knows you are rejecting his ideas, not him.

e. Reward openness with openness.

NONVERBAL TRUST EXERCISES

Taking a risk which makes you vulnerable to another person and receiving support can take place in a variety of nonverbal as well as verbal ways. One of the interesting aspects of the development of trust in a relationship is that sometimes the sense of physical support can be as powerful a developer of trust as a sense of emotional support. Your group may like to try some of the following nonverbal exercises. Each of them is related to the development of trust. Before you attempt the exercises, however, you should carefully consider the following points:

1. No one with a bad back or another physical condition that might be adversely affected should participate in an exercise in which they might be roughly handled.

2. Although these nonverbal exercises can be used as a form of play, they should be used only for educational purposes. That is, they should be done for a specific learning purpose, such as learning more about the development of trust, and they should be discussed thoroughly after they have been done.

3. Do not enter into an exercise unless you plan to behave in a trustworthy manner. If you cannot be trusted to support another person, do not enter into an exercise where you are responsible for physically supporting him. No one should be allowed to fall or to suffer any injury.

4. No group pressure should be exerted upon individuals to participate. Participation should be strictly voluntary. If you do not feel like volunteering, however, you may find it interesting to analyze why. You may learn something about yourself and your relationships with the other members of the group from such an analysis. A lack of trust in the group or in other individuals might lead you to refuse to participate; on the other hand, a sense of adventure and fun might lead you

to volunteer even though you do not trust the group or other individuals.

TRUST CIRCLE

The group stands facing into a close circle. A volunteer, or a person who wishes to develop more trust in the group, is handed around the inside of the circle by the shoulders and upper torso. He should stand with his feet in the center of the circle, close his eyes, and let the group pass him around or across their circle. His feet should not move from the center of the circle. After as many people who want to try it have been passed around the circle, discuss the following questions:

1. How did it feel to be on the inside of the circle? What were you thinking about; what was the experience like?
2. How did it feel to be a part of the circle, passing others around? What were you thinking about; what were you experiencing? Did you feel differently with different people in the center? Did the group behave differently when different people were in the center?
3. Some groups take a great deal of care in passing a person around and are very gentle; other groups engage in aggressive play and toss the person from side to side. What did your group do? What does it signify about the group and the members?

TRUST WALK

Each member of the group pairs up with another person. One person is designated as the guide, the other as a blind person. The blind person should close his eyes and the guide will lead him around the room. The guide should grasp the wrists of the blind person and either from the side or from behind guide the blind person around the room, planning as "rich" an experience as possible for the blind person using all the other senses besides sight. Touching experiences such as feeling the wall, the covering of a chair, the hair or face of another person are all interesting. If you can go outdoors, standing in the sun or the wind is enjoyable. In a large room trust in the guide can be tested by running across the room, the blind person keeping his eyes shut. After 15 minutes, reverse roles and repeat. After both individuals have been a guide and a blind person, discuss the following questions in the group as a whole:

1. How did it feel to be the blind person?

2. What were some of the best experiences your guide gave you?

3. What did you learn about the guide?

4. What did you learn about the blind person?

5. How did it feel to be the guide?

6. At this point, how do the two of you feel about each other?

TRUST CRADLE

The group forms two lines by the side of a volunteer. The volunteer leans back and the group picks him up, someone supporting his head. The volunteer should close his eyes and relax as much as possible. The group rocks him forwards and backwards. Slowly the group raises the person up, rocking him all the time, until he is as high as they can lift him. The group then slowly lowers the person to the floor, rocking him back and forth all the time. This can be repeated with several or all of the members of the group, depending upon the amount of time available. Afterwards, the group as a whole should discuss the following questions:

1. How did it feel to be cradled? What were you thinking of while the group was cradling you? What were you experiencing?

2. How did it feel to cradle the different members of the group? Did you have different feelings with different people?

3. How has trust in the group been affected by the experience?

TRUST FALL

Partners stand, one with his back turned to the other's front. With his arms extended sideways, he falls backwards and is caught by his partner. Reverse roles and repeat. You may like to try the exercise with several different group partners. Then discuss in the group as a whole the following questions:

1. How did it feel to fall? Did you doubt that the other would really catch you?

2. How did it feel to catch your partner? Did you doubt that you would be able to catch him?

3. How has trust in the individuals who caught you been affected?

ELEVATED TRUST PASSING

The group lines up in a straight line, each person facing the back of the person in front of him. The person at the beginning of the line is lifted high and is passed over the top of the others to the end of the line, where he is slowly brought down. The person now at the head of the line is lifted high and is passed over the top of the others to the end of the line. If a group member does not wish to be passed, he moves to the end of the line when he finds himself at the head of the line. The exercise continues until all members have been lifted and passed.

1. How did it feel to be passed?
2. What were you thinking; what were you experiencing?
3. How did it feel to pass the other members of the group?
4. How has trust in the group been affected by the exercise?

DEVELOPING TRUST

The objectives for this exercise are for the members of the group to arrive at a summary statement concerning the ways in which trust can be built in a relationship. The procedure for the exercise is as follows:

1. Divide into groups of four.
2. Arrive at the 10 most important things a person can do to develop trust in a relationship. Take 20 minutes for this.
3. Share the results across the group.
4. As a whole, rank the 10 most important aspects of developing trust from the most important to the least important.

Did your list include any of the following: progressively disclosing oneself to the other person; making sure your behavior regarding the other person is consistent; following through on your commitments to the other person; expressing warmth and acceptance to the other person; avoiding being judgmental or evaluative concerning the other person; being trustworthy; being honest.

CHECKLIST OF SKILLS

On the following scales, circle the number which indicates your perception of your skills and knowledge at this time.

1. *I understand what trust is and is not.*

Don't   Fully
understand   1 : 2 : 3 : 4 : 5 : 6 : 7 : 8 : 9   understand

2. *I understand how trust is developed in a relationship.*

Don't   Fully
understand   1 : 2 : 3 : 4 : 5 : 6 : 7 : 8 : 9   understand

3. *I can see when another person is trusting me.*

Never   1 : 2 : 3 : 4 : 5 : 6 : 7 : 8 : 9   Always

4. *I can trust other individuals when it is appropriate.*

Never   1 : 2 : 3 : 4 : 5 : 6 : 7 : 8 : 9   Always

5. *In order to build trust I can take risks in self-disclosure.*

Never   1 : 2 : 3 : 4 : 5 : 6 : 7 : 8 : 9   Always

6. *In order to build trust I can respond to another person's risks with acceptance and support.*

Never   1 : 2 : 3 : 4 : 5 : 6 : 7 : 8 : 9   Always

7. *In order to build trust I can reciprocate another person's risks with self-disclosure.*

Never   1 : 2 : 3 : 4 : 5 : 6 : 7 : 8 : 9   Always

8. At this point, what skills do I need more practice on?

_____ Taking risks with self-disclosure.

_____ Responding with acceptance and support.

_____ Reciprocating another person's self-disclosure.

_____ Responding with warmth.

_____ Having my verbal statements, nonverbal cues, and behavior all communicate the same message.

_____ Communicating my trust in another person.

ANSWERS

Pages 45–46:   *1: a, d; 2: b, d; 3: b, c, e*

Page 48:   *1: c, d; 2: c; 3: a, c, d, j*

Page 50:   *1: +10, +10; 2: +25, −25; 3: −25, +25; 4: −10, −10*

Pages 54–55:   *1: b, c, e, g; 2: a, d, e*

Increasing Your
Communication Skills

chapter

4

Man is often described as a communicating animal. All human progress has been achieved through cooperative action which depends upon effective communication. Our daily lives are filled with one communication experience after another. Through communication people reach some understanding of each other, learn to like each other, influence one another, build trust, form and terminate relationships, and learn more about themselves and how other people perceive them. Through communication you learn to understand others as persons and to help others to understand you as a person. No discussion of interpersonal skills can overlook the skills of communicating effectively.

WHAT IS COMMUNICATION?

Communication is defined as a person sending a message to another individual with the conscious intent of evoking a response. A person says, "Good morning," and another person replies, "Hello." A father shakes his head, and a child stops reaching for a forbidden object. In our discussion of communication we shall refer to the communicator as the *sender* and the person at whom the message is aimed as the *receiver*. The *message* may be a verbal, nonverbal, or behavioral stimulus that the sender transmits to the receiver. The *channel* is the means of conveying the message to the receiver; the soundwaves of the voice, the lightwaves involved in seeing, words on a printed page are all examples of channels. In interpersonal communication each individual serves both as a sender and a receiver. The interpersonal communication process may be represented in Figure 4.1.

Figure 4.1 represents a model of the process of communication between two individuals. There are seven basic elements in this model which may be discussed separately:

1. The intentions, ideas, feelings of the sender and the behavior he selects to engage in, all of which lead to his sending a message which conveys some content.
2. The sender encoding his message by translating his ideas, feelings, and intentions into a message appropriate for transmission.
3. The transmission of the message to the receiver.
4. The channel through which the message is translated.
5. The receiver decoding the message by taking the stimuli received and interpreting their meaning. The interpretation of the meaning of a message depends upon the receiver's comprehension of the content of the message and the intentions of the sender.
6. The receiver responding internally to his interpretation of the message.
7. The amount of *noise* in the above steps. Noise is any element that interferes with the communication process. In the sender, noise can refer to such things as the attitudes, prejudices, or frame of reference of the sender and the inappropriateness of his language or other expression to the message. In the receiver noise refers to such things as the attitudes, background, and experiences of the receiver which affect the decoding process. In the channel noise refers to environmental sounds such as static or traffic, speech problems such as stammering, annoying or distracting mannerisms such as a tendency to mumble, or other distractions. To a large extent, the success of communication is determined by the degree to which noise is overcome or controlled.

Effective communication exists between two persons when the receiver interprets the sender's message in the same way the sender intended it. In effective communication the messages of the sender directly reflect his intentions and the interpretations by the receiver match the intentions of the sender. Effective communication can be accomplished by striving for the highest possible degree of accuracy with which the receiver correctly interprets the intentions of the sender and the meaning of the message.

Where do difficulties in effective communication arise? Why is it so common for two individuals not to understand each other? Perhaps the most recurring and basic source of misunderstandings between two per-

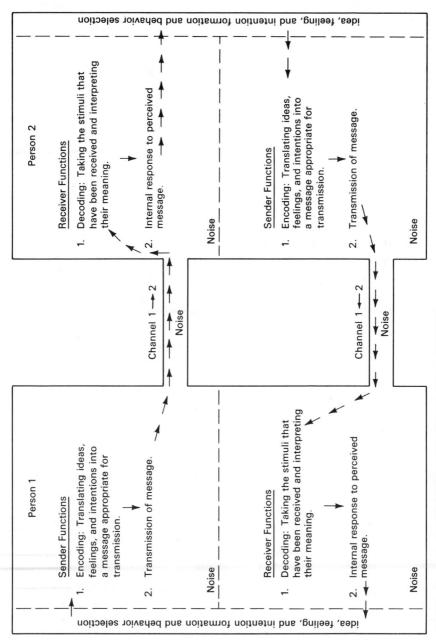

FIGURE 4.1 THE INTERPERSONAL COMMUNICATION PROCESS

sons are communication failures resulting from the receiver understanding the meaning of a message differently than it was intended. We do not always communicate what we mean to. Since intentions are private and known directly only to the person who experiences them, a sender's intentions are not always clear to the receiver. I know my intentions, but I must make inferences about yours. You know your intentions, but you must infer mine. Because of the private nature of intentions, difficulties in communication often result from the failure of the receiver to understand correctly the intentions of the sender.

The communication failures arising from the gap between what the sender meant and what the receiver thought the sender meant do not usually arise from word usage, grammatical form, or lack of verbal ability. Rather they are created by emotional and social sources of noise. People, for example, are often so preoccupied that they just do not listen to what others are saying. Or they can be so interested in what they have to say that they listen to others only to find an opening to get the floor to say what they want to say. Sometimes individuals are so sure that they know what the other person is going to say that they distort his statements to match their expectations—for example, when a boy who has a very low opinion of himself asks a girl for a date and takes her statement, "Let me think for a minute," as a refusal.

Sometimes individuals listen in order to evaluate and make judgments about the speaker, which in turn makes the speaker guarded and defensive in what he is trying to say. An example of this is when a person is presenting an argument and the receiver is constantly saying, "That's stupid; that's wrong." The speaker then becomes very careful about what he is saying. At times individuals do fully understand the words a communicator is using without understanding the real meaning of what he is trying to say—for example, when a person says, "It's a nice day," in an attempt to change the subject, and the receiver thinks the speaker is really interested in the weather. All of these problems in communication will be discussed more fully later in the chapter.

Finally, a lack of trust seems to act as a principle cause of communication distortion. Distrust can cause a reduction of the information shared and a suspiciousness of what little information is communicated. To a certain extent, increasing the communication between two individuals results in greater accuracy of understanding only when trust is high.

When you stop to think of how many ways individuals can misunderstand each other, it seems at times a wonder that any effective communication can take place at all. But in the exercise in this chapter we will examine and practice communication skills that promote effective, accurate understanding of each other's communications.

You may test your understanding of the material in this section by answering the following questions. (Answers are on p. 83.)

1. Which of the following are examples of communication according to the definition given?
   a. A lecture class where all the students are asleep.
   b. A little old lady hitting a burglar over the head with her umbrella.
   c. A mountain climber listening to his echo.
   d. You, reading this book and trying to answer this question.

2. What are the seven basic elements of communication?
   a. The subject of the conversation, around which all communication occurs.
   b. The intentions of the communicator.
   c. The receiver's reactions to the sender.
   d. Encoding.
   e. Transmission of the message.
   f. The receiver's understanding of the content of the message and the intention of the sender.
   g. The preferred style of thinking of the sender.
   h. The channel through which the message is sent.
   i. The internal response of the receiver.
   j. Noise.
   k. The categories of response the receiver has in his mind.
   l. Expressing acceptance and support.

3. When is there communication failure?
   a. When the communicator doesn't know what to say.
   b. When the receiver understands the message differently than it was meant.
   c. When the telephone lines are out of order.

4. What are some common communication faults of the receiver?
   a. Not giving the sender his undivided attention.
   b. Turning off his hearing aid.
   c. Relating the conversation to something the speaker does not know about.
   d. Thinking about his replies instead of paying attention to the sender.
   e. Listening for details rather than the essential message.
   f. Listening to the essential message but missing details.

SENDING MESSAGES EFFECTIVELY

What can you do to ensure effective communication of your ideas and feelings? In this and the following three chapters we will discuss the answer to this question. There are, however, several things the sender of a message can do to increase the likelihood that he will be accurately understood. They involve three dimensions—credibility of the sender, sending understandable messages, and ensuring optimal feedback on the effects your message is having on the receiver. In this section the first two dimensions will be briefly discussed. In the following section feedback will be covered.

A sender may do a series of things in order to increase the likelihood of his message being accurately understood. They include:

1. Increasing the redundancy of the message (and reducing the noise) by using more than one channel of communication (such as pictures and written messages as well as spoken words) and repeating the message more than once.

2. Making the message complete and specific, giving all the background information the receiver needs to understand your frame of reference and viewpoint.

3. Claiming your message as your own by using the personal pronouns *I* and *my,* and clearly taking responsibility for the ideas and feelings you express.

4. Ensuring that your verbal statements, nonverbal cues, and behavior are all congruent.

Probably the single most important element in interpersonal communication is the credibility of the sender. *Sender credibility* refers to the attitude the receiver has towards the trustworthiness of the sender's statements. Several dimensions affect the credibility of the sender:

1. Expertness relevant to the topic under discussion.

2. Reliability as an information source; this refers to the perceived character of the sender such as his dependability, predictability, and consistency.

3. Intentions of the sender. It is usually important for the receiver to know whether the motives of the sender are entirely selfish or not. Whatever effect we want our message to have upon the receiver, we should be open about it.

4. The expression of warmth and friendliness.

5. Dynamism of the sender. A dynamic sender is perceived to be aggressive, emphatic, and forceful. A dynamic sender tends to be perceived as more credible than is a passive sender.

6. The majority opinion of other people concerning the credibility of the sender. If all our friends tell us the sender is trustworthy, we tend to believe it.

There is little evidence available from the studies on sender credibility to suggest which of the above dimensions is most important. It seems, however, that a highly credible sender is one who is perceived in a favorable light on *all* of these dimensions. A source low in credibility, on the other hand, is one who is perceived in a negative light on *any one* of the dimensions. It seems advisable, therefore, for the sender to increase his credibility on all dimensions. Unless we appear credible to the receiver he will discount our message and we will not be able to communicate effectively with him. Sender credibility is often discussed as the perceived trustworthiness of the sender; therefore credibility relates to our discussion of trust in Chapter 3.

ONE- AND TWO-WAY COMMUNICATION EXERCISE [1]

One of the best ways for a sender to ensure the accuracy with which the receiver understands the sender's message is to obtain optimal feedback on the effects his message is having on the receiver. Feedback is the process by which the sender perceives how his message is being decoded and received. The response the receiver makes to the sender's message can subsequently cause the sender to modify his messages to communicate more accurately with the receiver. If the sender is not able to obtain information on how his message is being decoded, inaccuracies in communication may occur and never be uncovered. The primary means by which misunderstandings can be corrected is through obtaining feedback on how the receiver is interpreting the sender's message. Such open, two-way communication facilitates accuracy of understanding in communication, which in turn improves such things as developing a fulfilling relationship and being able to work together effectively.

One-way communication occurs when the sender is not able to determine how the receiver is decoding the sender's message. *Two-way* communication occurs when the sender is able to obtain feedback concerning how the receiver is decoding the sender's message. In this exercise we will compare one- and two-way communication. The objective is to demonstrate the differences between a situation in which two-way communication exists and ones in which communication goes only one way. For this exercise each participant needs two pieces of paper and a pencil. The leader needs copies of "Square Arrangement I" (p. 239) and "Square Arrangement II" (p. 241), and he should copy Tables 4.1A–C onto a blackboard or a large sheet of newsprint. The procedure for the exercise is as follows:

[1] This exercise is adapted from an excercise in Harold J. Leavitt, *Managerial Psychology*, (University of Chicago Press, 1958), pp. 118–28.

1. The leader selects a sender and two observers (if the group has less than seven members select only one observer). The sender should be a person who communicates well and who speaks clearly and loudly enough to be heard.

2. The sender is seated either with his back to the group or behind a screen. He is given "Square Arrangement I." The leader should be careful that the group members do not see the diagram of squares which the sender will describe. The sender is told to study the first arrangement carefully for two minutes in order to be prepared to instruct the group members on how to draw a similar set of squares on their paper.

3. The first observer is asked to note the behavior and reactions of the sender during the exercise and to make notes for later comment. The second observer is asked to make notes on the behavior and reactions of the group members. Facial reactions, gestures, posture, and other nonverbal behaviors may be observed.

4. The group is given these instructions: "The sender is going to describe a drawing to you. You are to listen carefully to his instructions and draw what he describes as accurately as you can. You will be timed, but there is no time limit. *You may ask no questions of the sender and give no audible response.* You are asked to work independently."

5. The Tables 4.1A–C (p. 70) are placed in the front of the room. The sender is then told to proceed to give the instructions for drawing the first figure of squares as quickly and accurately as he can. The leader should ensure that there are no questions or audible reactions from the group members.

6. When the sender has completed giving the instructions for "Square Arrangement I," the leader records the time it took to do so in the proper space in the first table. Each member of the group is asked to write down on his paper the number of squares he thinks he has drawn correctly in relation to the preceding one.

7. The leader instructs the sender to face the group members. He gives the sender "Square Arrangement II" and tells him to study the relationship of the squares in this new diagram for two minutes in preparation for instructing the group members on how to draw it.

8. The group is given these instructions: "The sender is going to describe another drawing to you. This time he will be in full view of you and you may ask him as many questions as you wish. He is free to reply to your questions or amplify his statements as he sees fit. He is not, however, allowed to make any hand signals while describing the drawing. You will be timed, but there is no time limit. Work as accurately and rapidly as you can."

9. The sender is told to proceed.

10. When the sender has completed giving instructions for the second figure, the time is again recorded in the appropriate space of Table 4.1A. The group members are asked to guess the number of squares they have drawn correctly and to record the number on their papers.

11. A median for guessed accuracy on the first drawing is obtained by recording the number of group members who guessed zero, the number who guessed one, and so on in Table 4.1B. The median guessed number is found by counting from zero the number of group members guessing each number until you reach half the members of the group. The median is then recorded in Table 4.1A.

12. The same method is repeated to get the median of accurate guesses for the second drawing.

13. Members are shown the master drawing for the first set of squares and the relationship of each square to the preceding one is pointed out. Each square must be in the exact relationship to the preceding one as it appears on the master drawing to be counted as correct. When this has been completed, the members are asked to count and record the actual number right. A similar count is taken for the second chart.

14. The median for accuracy for the first and second drawings is obtained and placed in Table 4.1A.

15. The following questions are discussed:
    a. What may be concluded from the results in terms of time, accuracy, and level of confidence?
    b. What did the observers record during the exercise? How did the behavior of the sender and the group members vary from one situation to the other? The group members and the sender should comment on what they were feeling during the two situations.
    c. How does this exercise compare with situations you find yourself in at work, school, or at home? How might you change your behavior in relating to your friends and acquaintances as a result of what you have experienced during this exercise?

The typical result of this exercise is that one-way communication is quicker, less accurate, and the level of confidence of the receiver is lower. Two-way communication takes more time, but it also is likely to be more accurate and the level of confidence of the receiver is higher. The sender, however, usually is more disturbed and frustrated during the two-way communication process.

Just as the sender can increase the accuracy of communication by transmitting his message through a variety of channels, it is also an aid to accuracy if feedback is available in a variety of channels. Feedback does not have to be only verbal; the nonverbal cues such as facial expression, posture, gestures, sighs, tone of voice when asking questions, and so on are often indicative of how your message is being interpreted by the receiver.

TABLE 4.1A   MEDIANS FOR TRIALS I AND II

Medians	I	II
Time Elapsed:	_____	_____
Guess Accuracy:	_____	_____
Actual Accuracy:	_____	_____

TABLE 4.1B   FIRST TRIAL

Number Correct	Guess	Actual
5	_____	_____
4	_____	_____
3	_____	_____
2	_____	_____
1	_____	_____
0	_____	_____

TABLE 4.1C   SECOND TRIAL

Number Correct	Guess	Actual
5	_____	_____
4	_____	_____
3	_____	_____
2	_____	_____
1	_____	_____
0	_____	_____

EXERCISES FOR INCREASING
YOUR COMMUNICATION SKILLS

You are about to receive instructions for a series of experiences dealing with effective and ineffective communication. These experiences will provide you with the opportunity (1) to become more aware of effective and ineffective communication procedures, (2) to become more aware of your own behavior in communicating with others, (3) to practice effective communication procedures in order to develop increased skills. Such increased awareness and skill practice will increase your ability to develop and maintain effective interpersonal skills.

The suggested procedures at first may seem deceptively simple. Once you attempt to do them, however, you may find them more difficult than you expected. You will also find that the recommended procedures are very powerful when skillfully used. If you become involved in the exercise, and consciously attempt both to learn as much as possible and to enjoy yourself, you will develop considerably better communication skills. If you try the activities willingly and with enthusiasm, you can have a lot of fun while learning.

The steps of the following exercise, adapted from an exercise developed by Alan Anderson, are designed to lead you from a situation in which you conduct an irrelevant, somewhat destructive conversation to a situation in which you use the tools of communicating effectively in building more personal relationships. The exercise serves the following purposes:

1. It allows you to experience two types of conversation that interfere with developing personal relationships and two kinds of conversation that facilitate development of personal relationships.

2. It provides skill practice in how to listen effectively and to respond to messages sent by another person.

3. It provides skill practice in how to send effectively messages that facilitate the development of close personal relationships.

4. It introduces several key concepts on communication, such as (a) listening with understanding, (b) selective perception, (c) personal statements, and (d) relationship statements.

The session consists of three steps. The first two steps will contrast effective with ineffective ways of listening and responding. The final step will permit effective listening and responding in a situation emphasizing effective ways of sending messages. In each step a combination of experience, theory, and discussion will be used. At the end, a summary will be given and further skill development will be discussed.

All communication affects the relationship between the sender and the receiver. It either moves the relationship forward, backward, or keeps it the same. Communication can deepen a relationship or it can make the relationship more distant and impersonal. Many problems found in close relationships stem from failures to communicate effectively. The following experiences will illustrate the skills involved in deepening relationships by communication.

For the following activities you will need a partner and two more people to make groups of two and four. Communication is not a solitary activity, so find three other individuals and proceed.

STEP ONE: NO LISTENING VERSUS CLOSELY LISTENING; IRRELEVANT RESPONSE VERSUS RELEVANT RESPONSE

Part 1: Discussion on Listening. What types of problems make it difficult for two persons to understand each other? What failures in sending, listening, and responding cause communication gaps? List below at least four reasons why two persons may fail to communicate with each other.

1. _____

2. _____

3. _____

4. _____

Do your suggestions include the following?

1. Inaccurate expression of one's thoughts.
2. Failing to listen to all that is being said.
3. Trying to say too much in one statement.
4. Two individuals not talking about the same thing while they are in a conversation with each other.

Part 2: No Listening and Irrelevant Response. Divide into groups of four.

1. Conduct a discussion on establishing close friendships or relating to others. Allow five minutes of discussion. During the discussion, you must talk about the assigned topic and what you say must be unrelated to what others in the group say. It is as though you did not hear them.

2. After the discussion, jot down answers to the following questions to use later:

a. How did it feel to make a statement and have no one respond to it?

_____

_____

_____

b. How did it feel to ignore a statement made by others in the group?

_____

_____

_____

Part 3: Close Listening and Relevant Response. Within the group of four divide into pairs. Designate one member of each pair *A*, the other *B*.

1. *A* makes a statement to *B* either about himself, about *B*, or about the relationship between them. Try not to make bland statements, but say something that you have some feelings about and that can have real meaning for both of you.

2. *B* paraphrases *A*'s statement, stating in his own words what *A*'s remark meant to him. There is to be no discussion of the statements. *A* simply makes the statement; *B* paraphrases it back. Some general rules for paraphrasing response are:
   a. Restate the other person's expressed feelings and ideas in your own words; don't mimic or parrot the exact words of the other person.
   b. Preface reflected remarks with, "You feel . . . ," "You think . . . ," "It seems to you that . . . ," "It sometimes appears to you that . . . ," and so on.
   c. In paraphrasing another person's statements, avoid any indication of approval or disapproval. Refrain from blaming, interpreting, giving advice, or persuading.

3. *A* makes a second statement to *B*. *B* paraphrases it.

4. *A* makes a third statement to *B*. *B* paraphrases it.

5. Reverse the process. *B* makes three statements to *A;* after each one *A* paraphrases it back.

6. Jot down answers to the following questions to use later:
   a. How did it feel to make a statement and have your partner paraphrase it?

_____

_____

_____

b. How did it feel to paraphrase a statement made by your partner?

_____

_____

_____

7. Discuss your experiences in the group of four. Some questions you may use to facilitate the discussion are:
   a. Did you find that you had difficulty in listening to others during the exercise? Why?
   b. Did you find that you were not getting across what you wanted to say?
   c. What was your reaction to the paraphrasing of your partner? Was he receiving what you intended to send?
   d. Was the manner of presentation by your partner affecting your listening ability? In what way?
   e. What were the differences in your feelings during the two types of experiences?

Part 4: Theory on Listening and Responding. To speak precisely and to listen carefully presents a challenge. Some of the common faults in communication are as follows: The sender does not organize his thoughts before speaking; he includes too many ideas, often unrelated, in his message and thus makes comprehension difficult; and he ignores answering points made by the previous sender and therefore does not actually respond to what has been said. The receiver often does not give his undivided attention; he keeps thinking about his answers instead of paying full attention; and he tends to listen for details rather than for the essential message.

The way in which you listen and respond to another person is crucial for building a fulfilling relationship. You can either listen and respond in ways that make the relationship more distant and impersonal, or you can listen and respond in ways that bring you and the sender into a closer, more personal relationship. It is crucial in a close relationship for you to communicate that you have clearly heard and understood the sender. It is characteristic of impersonal relationships that the receiver communicates that he has not heard and has not understood the sender. When you listen accurately and respond relevantly, you communicate to the sender, "I care about what you are saying, and I want to understand it." When you fail to listen and respond irrelevantly, you communicate to the sender, "I don't care about what you are saying, and I don't want to understand it." The previous experiences have highlighted the two different ways of listening and responding.

There are other ways of listening and responding that alienate the sender (Rogers and Roethlisberger, 1952; Roger, 1965). Perhaps the major barrier to building close relationships is the very natural tendency we have to judge, evaluate, approve, or disapprove of the statements made by the sender. This happens when the sender makes a statement and you respond internally or openly with, "I think you're wrong," "I don't like what you said," "I think your views are right," or "I agree entirely."

Although the tendency to give evaluative responses is common in almost all conversations, it is very much heightened in situations where feelings and emotions are deeply involved. The stronger the feelings, the more likely that two persons will each evaluate the other's statements from only his own point of view.

More effective communication occurs, and this evaluative tendency is avoided, when the receiver gives understanding responses (paraphrases). An understanding response not only communicates desire to understand the sender without evaluating his statements; it also helps the receiver to see the expressed ideas and feelings from the sender's point of view. When paraphrasing is skillfully done, the receiver is able to achieve the sender's frame of reference in regard to the message. Although paraphrasing sounds simple, it is often very difficult to do. Yet it has powerful effects. Many counselors and psychotherapists have found that listening intently to what a person says, understanding how it seems to him, seeing the personal flavor which it has for him, is very helpful to the sender. If you paraphrase a message, that act tends to reduce the sender's fears about revealing himself to you and decreases the sender's defensiveness about what he is communicating. It facilitates psychological health and growth. There is every indication that such empathetic understanding is such an effective approach to building close interpersonal relationships that it can bring about major positive changes in personality.

How do you improve your skills in listening empathetically to others? One way is simply to follow this rule the next time you get deeply involved in a conversation or argument: *Each person can speak up for himself only after he has first restated the ideas and feelings of the previous sender accurately and to the sender's satisfaction.* This means that before presenting your own point of view, it would be necessary for you to achieve the other's frame of reference, to understand his thoughts and feelings so well that you could paraphrase them for him. Sounds simple? Try it; you will find that it is one of the most difficult things you ever attempted. You will also find that your arguments will become much more constructive and productive if you are able to follow the above rule successfully.

You may wish to assess your comprehension of the above material by answering the following questions (answers on p. 83):

1. What is the effect of judgmental or evaluative responses on communication?
   a. They increase the accuracy of communication.
   b. They encourage the sender to elaborate on his statements.
   c. They increase the sender's fears about disclosing his ideas and feelings to the receiver.
   d. They spice up the conversation.
   e. They increase the sender's defensiveness about what he is saying.
   f. They alienate the sender.

2. Three rules for effective paraphrasing are:
   a. Repeat the sender's words exactly and with the same inflections.
   b. Restate the sender's message in your own words.
   c. Preface your paraphrasing with such remarks as, "You feel . . ."
   d. Indicate whether you approve or disapprove of his message.
   e. Do not indicate any approval or disapproval of the sender's statements.

3. How does giving an understanding response, a paraphrase, facilitate communication?
   a. It helps the receiver to see the expressed ideas and feelings from the sender's frame of reference.
   b. It communicates to the sender that the receiver cares about the message and wants to understand it.
   c. It increases the amount of time two individuals talk with each other.

STEP TWO: PARTIAL LISTENING VERSUS LISTENING FOR MEANING; ASYNDETIC RESPONSE VERSUS ATTENDING AND NEGOTIATING FOR MEANING RESPONSE

Part 1: Partial Listening and Asyndetic Responding. Divide into groups of four.

1. Conduct a discussion about establishing a close friendship, relating to others, or some other related topic. Discuss the topic for five minutes.

2. This time you are to listen to what the others say but only for the purpose of using some small part of what they said in order to change the discussion to something more interesting to you. In other words, you acknowledge their statement but use it only as a polite way of introducing your own ideas into the conversation. This is called an asyndetic response.

3. Jot down answers to the following questions for use in a later discussion:

a. How did it feel having others change the subject right after your statement?

_____

_____

_____

b. How did it feel changing the subject right after others had made a statement?

_____

_____

_____

Part 2: Listening for Meaning and Attending and Negotiating for Meaning Response. Divide into pairs. Designate one person *A,* the other *B.*

1. *A* makes a statement about himself, about *B,* or about their relationship.
2. *B* responds by saying, "What I think you mean is . . ." (He then says what he thinks *A* meant.) He does not try to speculate about why he thinks that or about why *A* might be saying that. He simply tells *A* exactly what he thinks *A* meant by the statement. *A* and *B* then negotiate until they are in complete agreement about what *A* really meant and *A* is able to respond to *B* with, "Yes, that is exactly what I meant." Do not add to or go beyond the original meaning, and don't try to analyze each other. Simply attempt to get at the exact meaning of what was said.
3. *A* makes a second statement. *B* responds with, "What I think you mean is . . ." The two then negotiate the exact meaning of the statement.
4. *A* makes a third statement. *B* responds as before.
5. Reverse the process. *B* makes three statements and *A* responds.
6. Answer these questions:
   a. How did it feel to make a statement and have my partner reply with what he thought it meant, then for us to negotiate the exact meaning of the statement?

   _____

   _____

   _____

b. How did it feel to listen to my partner's statements and respond with what I thought it meant, then for us to negotiate the exact meaning of the statements?

_____

_____

_____

7. Discuss the experiences in your group of four. Some questions you may use in the discussion are:
   a. Did you always communicate what you wanted to communicate?
   b. Did you find the listener only responding to part of what you said?
   c. Was it ever unclear what the speaker had in mind? What made it unclear?

Part 3: Theory on Selective Perception in Listening and Responding. Did you notice that in responding to your partner's statement you selected part of his message to respond to and did not respond to other parts? This is very common in communication. It is based on the fact that our perceptions have to be selective. A message has too many aspects, both verbal and nonverbal, for a receiver to respond to all of them. Even when a person says, "How are you?" a receiver may ignore the tone of voice, facial expression, gestures of the sender, and the appropriateness of the message to the situation; he may only respond to the usual meaning of the words. Most communication is so complex that we have to be selective about what we perceive and what we respond to. Selective perception, however, is one of the sources of "noise" in the communication process. Some of the factors which influence what we respond to in a message are our expectations, our needs, wants, and desires, and our opinions, attitudes, and beliefs.

If you expect a person to act unfriendly, you will be sensitive to anything that can be perceived as rejection and unfriendliness. If your past experience has led you to expect certain people to be hostile, you will be sensitive to any expression that can be seen as hostile. Such sensitization may make you completely blind to friendly expressions.

If you need and want someone to give you support, on the other hand, you may be highly sensitive to any expressions that can be perceived as supportive. If you are hungry you may be sensitive to any messages about food; or if you want to go home after a long evening you may be sensitive to how tired others are. Your wants and your needs constantly affect what you perceive in interpersonal communications situations.

Finally, there is evidence that you will be more sensitive to perceiving messages that are consistent with your opinions and attitudes. You will tend to misperceive or fail to perceive messages that are opposite to your opinions, beliefs, and attitudes. You learn and remember material that is consistent with your attitudes, beliefs, and opinions. In many ways your attitudes, beliefs, and opinions affect what you perceive in interpersonal communications.

In listening and responding appropriately to others, it is important to be aware of the likelihood of selectivity in what you perceive and to be ready to change your perceptions when it becomes evident that you have misperceived a message. Your interpretations of what messages mean will always be tentative until confirmed by the sender; this is one reason why it is so important to negotiate the meaning of a message before you respond to it.

You may wish to answer the following questions to see how well you understood the content of this section (answers on p. 83):

1. What is selective perception?
   a. Responding to all the aspects, both verbal and nonverbal, of a message.
   b. Responding only to a few of the verbal and nonverbal aspects of a message.
   c. The name of a famous race horse.

2. Which of the following are factors that influence selective perception?
   a. Self-disclosure.
   b. Expectations.
   c. The weather.
   d. Needs, wants, desires.
   e. Opinions, attitudes, beliefs.
   f. Trust.

3. How can you avoid misunderstandings due to selective perception?
   a. Do not try to communicate.
   b. Keep all interpretations of messages tentative until confirmed by the sender.
   c. Do not have expectations, needs, or opinions.

STEP THREE: THE USE OF EFFECTIVE COMMUNICATION SKILLS— CLARIFYING PERSONAL STRENGTHS AND CLARIFYING RELATIONSHIPS

Part 1: Clarifying Strengths.   Divide into pairs.

1. *A* takes two minutes to share with *B* what he considers to be his personal strengths, including things he thinks he does well, things he likes about himself, and things he thinks others like about him.
2. *B* "bombards" *A* with any observations he has about *A*'s strengths and

personal assets. In each case, when *A* receives an item of feedback he responds (a) by paraphrasing the feedback and (b) by stating what he thinks *B* means and negotiating the meaning. Do not take more than five minutes to do this.

3. Reverse roles and repeat the same process.

Part 2: Personal Statements. *Personal statements* are messages referring to yourself—about what you are feeling, what you are doing, what you are thinking, how you see yourself and your behavior, and so on. Whenever you refer to yourself the discussion target is called "personal." The hallmark of personal statements are the pronouns, *I, me,* and *my.* Using general words such as *everyone* or *some people* to refer to your ideas and feelings confuses the receivers and results in miscommunications and poor understanding. Personal statements reveal who you are to the receiver. They increase the personal quality of the relationship. One of the primary ways in which a sender can ensure clear communication is to make personal statements. Personal statements provide the receiver with a clearer idea of the sender's intentions than do impersonal statements and therefore offer less possibility of being misunderstood.

New personal statements also communicate personal involvement and trust in the relationship. Using general words to refer to your feelings and ideas is a symptom of mistrust; it is usually when you are mistrustful and defensive that you are afraid to "own" your feelings and ideas. The openness and trust communicated by personal statements increases the possibilities of a closer friendship developing between the sender and the receiver.

With your partner, decide which of the following are personal statements (answers on p. 83):

1. I love you.
2. I hate you.
3. You are a beautiful person.
4. You have big feet.
5. We communicate well together.
6. I feel nervous when you look at me that way.
7. You make people feel good just by smiling at them.

Then discuss with your partner the following questions:

1. In making statements about your strengths, to what extent were the statements clearly personal statements?
2. What is your reaction to making personal statements and to receiving personal statements?

3. How do you think personal statements facilitate the development of a relationship and improve communication between the sender and the receiver?

Part 3: Clarifying Relationships. Divide into pairs.

1. Person *A* says, "One thing which you could do to improve our relationship is . . ."
2. Person *B* (a) paraphrases the statement and (b) states what he thinks *A* meant by the statement; they then negotiate its meaning. Once the meaning is clearly agreed upon, *B* states, "My reaction to that is . . ."
3. Repeat the process.
4. Reverse roles and repeat steps 1–3.

Part 4: Relationship Statements. *Relationship statements* are messages expressing what you think or feel about another person. Whenever two or more individuals talk about what they think or feel about each other, the discussion target is called "relationship." The topic of discussion is the relationship among the individuals involved. Relationship statements change the relationship; they consider clearly where the relationship is and what needs to happen in order for it to develop.

Many individuals spend so much time together they automatically become friends or enemies. But relationships do not "just happen"; they are built. They can be built consciously or unconsciously. When one is attempting to build a relationship, the more conscious he is about where the relationship is and what needs to happen for it to become more personal, the greater the possibilities of a close friendship resulting. Making relationship statements clarifies where two individuals stand and facilitates the expression of feelings and perceptions that can lead to a deeper, more satisfying relationship.

When you are trying to develop a friendship, relationship statements can be used to deepen the relationship. When you send messages to the receiver, there is less chance of misunderstanding if you are open with your statements and relate them to the present nature of the relationship and how you see the other person. Through learning how to make relationship statements you can learn how to work consciously to deepen your relationship and minimize the chances of miscommunication while you are doing so.

With your partner, decide which of the following are relationship statements (answers on p. 83):

1. I feel you are rejecting me.
2. The old town just isn't the same anymore.

3. You really make me feel liked and appreciated.

4. This group really bugs me.

5. Everyone here is so nice.

6. Are you angry with me?

7. Why is everyone looking at me?

8. I think we need to talk about what happened last night.

Discuss the following questions with your partner:

1. How do you feel about making relationship statements?

2. In making statements about your relationship, which of the statements were most helpful in the development of your relationship and how were they helpful?

EXERCISE ON OBSERVING COMMUNICATION BEHAVIOR

You have just been through a series of short experiences on effective and ineffective communication behavior. You may wish to sharpen your skills in recognizing such behavior. The procedure for this exercise is as follows:

1. Pick a group to observe, or sit down in a crowded area in which a number of conversations are going on.

2. Using the observations sheets found on pp. 243 and 245, count the number of times each type of effective or ineffective communication behavior takes place.

3. In a week's time, discuss in the group the results of your observations. What general conclusions can you draw from what the members of your group observed?

TOWARD IMPROVED COMMUNICATION SKILLS

The difficulties in establishing meaningful communication between individuals are very real. What, then, can be done to improve understanding? One thing is the development of an atmosphere of mutual confidence and trust through the use of personal and relationship statements. Secondly, the use of communication skills such as paraphrasing, negotiating meaning, and making your responses relevant to the sender's message all improve understanding. You may also facilitate the development of close, personal relationships by making your messages reflect personal and relationship statements and by making your responses reflect a recognition of the other person's strengths and capabilities. Through the use of such skills you can consciously maximize the possibilities of developing close, fulfilling relationships with other people.

CHECKLIST OF SKILLS

1. I have mastered the following:

_____ Understanding (paraphrasing) response.

_____ Negotiating for meaning response.

_____ Personal statements.

_____ Relationship statements.

_____ Responding in ways which confirm the other person's strengths.

_____ Recognizing when ineffective communication is taking place.

_____ Recognizing when effective communication is taking place.

_____ Engaging in two-way communication.

2. I need more work on:

_____ Understanding (paraphrasing) response.

_____ Negotiating for meaning response.

_____ Personal statements.

_____ Relationship statements.

_____ Responding in ways which confirm the other person's strengths.

_____ Recognizing when ineffective communication is taking place.

_____ Recognizing when effective communication is taking place.

_____ Engaging in two-way communication.

ANSWERS

Page 65:   1: b, d; 2: b, d, e, f, h, i, j; 3: b; 4: a, d, e
Page 76:   1: c, e, f; 2: b, c, e; 3: a, b
Page 79:   1: b; 2: b, d, e; 3: b
Page 80:   1, 2, 6
Pages 81–82:   1, 3, 6, 8

The Verbal Expression
of Feelings

Falling in love, making friendships, experiencing the warmth and intimacy of close personal friendships are some of the most exciting aspects of being alive. Much of human society and human action seems based upon the liking individuals have for one another. The words that name aspects of interpersonal attraction, such as *like, love, dislike,* and *hate,* are among the most frequently used in the English language. Liking for another person may be defined as simply your predisposition to respond towards a particular person in a favorable manner.

INTERPERSONAL FRIENDSHIPS

In order to be friends, two people must know and like each other. In order to make friends, you must like the other person and the other person must like you. This means spending time together and getting to know each other. In addition, there are at least three ways in which mutual liking may be developed. The first is getting involved in a mutual project where cooperation is necessary. We like those people with whom we are involved in cooperative action. The second is maximizing the mutual perceptions of similarity in terms of attitudes, values, beliefs, background, interests, and personality. We tend to like those people who are similar to us. Since there are no interpersonal skills involved in either of these ways of increasing mutual liking, they will not be discussed here. The third way is for you to express liking towards the other person; he, in turn, will tend to reciprocate your feelings.

We tend to like those people who like us and to dislike those people who dislike us. By expressing liking for another person, you create a situation in which he will probably feel affection and liking for you. In order to build a close, personal relationship you must like the other person and he must like you, and this liking must be clearly communicated to each other. Since liking tends to be reciprocated, the clear communication of liking will tend to increase the other person's liking for you.

Yet how do we tell if someone likes us? How do we communicate our liking for another person to that person? To like someone is to feel affection, warmth, caring for that person. The expression of a feeling such as warmth is probably the most powerful indication of liking available. To express liking for another person, therefore, you must be able to clearly communicate your feelings of warmth to that person. In this and the following chapter we will focus upon how feelings can be constructively and clearly communicated to other individuals.

EXPRESSION OF WARMTH

There is overwhelming evidence that the expression of warmth results in positive attitudes towards the expresser (Johnson, 1971b). The warmth you express towards another person is significantly related to being liked and trusted, to being perceived as similar (both as a person and in beliefs and values), to being seen as being accepting of the other person and of his beliefs and attitudes, and to being perceived as an understanding person. Thus the expression of warmth is one of the most powerful tools available for building and maintaining friendships with other individuals. In addition the expression of warmth is crucial to building a climate of acceptance and support in a relationship as well as a high level of interpersonal trust.

EXPRESSION OF FEELINGS OTHER THAN WARMTH

In any relationship there are many feelings other than warmth that are generated. Every relationship has periods of conflict; how they are handled is vitally important for building and maintaining a close friendship. In a conflict, the expression of anger and other emotions other than warmth may be necessary to clear the air and reach an understanding. To be genuine and authentic in a relationship will require a willingness to be open in communicating many emotions other than warmth and affection. This and the next chapter, therefore, will focus upon the constructive expression of any feelings, with special emphasis on the expression of warmth.

COMMUNICATION OF FEELINGS

Emotions and feelings are psychologically healthy. Experiencing emotions and expressing them to another person is desirable, necessary for your psychological well-being, and one of the major sources of joy and fun in your life. It is natural to have feelings. The capacity to feel is as much a part of being a person as is the capacity to think and reason. A person without feelings is not a person at all; he is a machine. The quest of individuals who really enjoy life is (1) how to feel a greater range of emotions and a wider variety of emotions and (2) how to build relationships where their emotions are aroused and are allowed positive expression. Feeling and expressing love for another person, feeling and expressing affection for another person, even feeling and expressing anger towards another person are all potentially highly rewarding and beautiful experiences. Feelings are potentially highly constructive since it is through experiencing and expressing feelings that close friendships are built and maintained.

Yet the way we express feelings and emotions is perhaps the most frequent source of difficulty in interpersonal relationships. Every individual continually experiences feelings about himself and others, but many individuals have not yet learned to accept and use their feelings constructively. A common source of difficulty in our relationships with others is the way in which we deal with our feelings, especially in our failure to use our feelings to create deeply personal relationships. Problems arise in interpersonal relationships, not because emotions are present, but because they are not used well. Individuals get into interpersonal difficulties because of mistaken attempts to repress, distort, or disguise their true feelings, not because they have feelings.

There are several difficulties in expressing feelings constructively in interpersonal relationships. One source of difficulty is that it is common for individuals to deny or ignore not only their own feelings but the feelings expressed by others as well. A typical response to someone who expresses a feeling is some variation of "don't feel that way." To a person expressing discouragement, depression, disappointment, we might say things like, "Cheer up!" "Don't let it get you down." "There's no use in crying over spilled milk." "Things will get better." All of these responses mean, "Don't feel that way." To a person in pain we might say, "Don't cry. Think of something pleasant." To an angry person we might say, "Simmer down. There's no point in getting angry. Let's be objective." To the person expressing joy or satisfaction in something he has accomplished we might say, "Better watch out; pride goeth before a fall." All of these statements communicate, "don't feel that way." Certainly you should avoid telling others to deny, repress, or ignore their feelings.

Another indication of the difficulty individuals often experience in dealing with feelings is that the more distant and remote the feelings, the more comfortably they discuss them. Do you, for example, find it easier to talk about feelings concerning someone else than about feelings toward persons who are present in a conversation? Does the following scale roughly represent the way in which most people you know deal with feelings?

Most Distant   *Least Difficult to Discuss*

I tell you how Jane felt about John,
  neither person being present.

I tell you how Jane feels about John,
  neither person being present.

I tell you my past feelings about Sam,
  who is not present.

I tell you my present feelings about
  Sam, who is not present.

I tell you my past feelings about you.

I tell you my present feelings about you.

Here and Now   *Most Difficult to Discuss*

In general, the closer the feelings are to dealing with you and me in the present moment the more difficult they are to discuss openly. Why is this so? Why are individuals uncomfortable with dealing with the present feelings of themselves and others? One reason is that such a self-disclosure is a risk that makes you vulnerable to being rejected by the other person. Another reason may be that once feelings are out in the open and recognized, you may feel that you are losing control of the relationship. If a person expresses love or anger towards another, for example, he cannot control what the other person's reactions may be. A third reason may be that the expression of feelings often implies a demand. If a person says, "You make me angry," he may be implicitly saying, "Stop doing what you are doing." Or if a person says, "I feel attracted to you," he may be implicitly saying, "Like me." Such demands expressed in feelings can precipitate a struggle for control between the two persons.

Finally, a difficulty in expressing feelings constructively in interpersonal situations is that many individuals do not recognize, much less accept, many of their own feelings. Without awareness of your feelings you cannot express them constructively. Unless you are aware of your feelings, accept them as natural and potentially constructive, and are skilled in the constructive expression of feelings, you may experience a great deal of difficulty in dealing with feelings in your interpersonal relationships. In this and the following chapter we will examine the skills involved in expressing feelings constructively.

To check your understanding of the above material, answer the following questions (answers on p. 101):

1. What are three ways in which liking may be developed in a relationship?
   a. Being agreeable.
   b. Getting involved in a cooperative project.
   c. Minimizing the areas of disagreement.
   d. Maximizing the mutual perceptions of similarity.
   e. Expressing liking toward the other person.
   f. Being totally honest.
2. Emotions and feelings are
   a. Nasty.
   b. Psychologically healthy.
   c. A source of joy and fun.
   d. Signs of difficulty in relating to other people.
3. Problems arise in relationships because
   a. Emotions and feelings are expressed.
   b. Of mistaken attempts to repress, distort, or disguise feelings.
4. What are four common sources of difficulty in expressing feelings constructively?
   a. Pronouncing words correctly.
   b. They are difficult to express.
   c. Expression of feelings implies a demand.
   d. Other people don't want you to express your feelings.
   e. Recognizing and accepting your feelings.
   f. Feeling a loss of control by being vulnerable to rejection.
   g. The risk in self-disclosure that makes you vulnerable to rejection.

CONSEQUENCES OF SUPPRESSING FEELINGS

There seems to be a normal attitude in our society that feelings interfere with a person's ability to handle interpersonal difficulties and to solve interpersonal problems. The assumption is that a person's interpersonal effectiveness increases as his behavior becomes more rational, logical, and objective. To the contrary, a person's interpersonal effectiveness increases as all the relevant information (including feelings) becomes conscious, discussable, and controllable. The suppression of feelings leads to ineffective interpersonal behavior. The expression of feelings is vital to effectively building a close friendship. If a person attempts to suppress the expression of feelings in a relationship, several consequences harmful to the relationship may result.

First, feelings that are unresolved and are not dealt with make for biased, nonobjective judgments and actions in interpersonal situations. It is quite common for a person to refuse to accept a good idea because a person he dislikes suggests it, or to accept a poor idea because a person he likes suggests it. A person may find himself withdrawing from a relationship because he is angry with the other person and therefore decides he doesn't like the other person any more. Situations such as this would not happen if individuals openly expressed their feelings and resolved them through interpersonal problem-solving.

Second, feelings that are unresolved and are not dealt with affect the person's perception of events and information in interpersonal situations. In Chapter Four selective perception was discussed. When feelings are unresolved, selective perception may occur; threatening and unpleasant facts are often denied, ignored, or distorted. Every person has blind spots where he misinterprets or ignores information because it is threatening or unpleasant. Unresolved feelings tend to increase your blind spots.

Finally, any relationship has to be maintained in good condition over time. Making a friend is just the beginning of a relationship. Maintaining the relationship calls for open expression of feelings so that any difficulties or conflicts can be dealt with in a productive way. The suppression of feelings can lead to barriers and increased conflicts, and, therefore, to a deterioration of the relationship.

WAYS OF EXPRESSING FEELINGS

There are three ways of communicating feelings: verbally, nonverbally, and tacitly through behavior. The congruency or agreement of your verbal, nonverbal, and tacit expression of feelings is important for clear communication. Many of the communication difficulties experienced in relationships spring from giving contradictory cues to other individuals when your actions, words, and nonverbal cues all indicate different feelings. To communicate your feelings effectively, your behavior, words, and nonverbal cues need to be congruent.

In this chapter we will focus upon the verbal ways in which feelings and emotions can be constructively communicated to other individuals because this is perhaps the easiest skill to develop. In the next chapter we will focus upon the nonverbal ways in which feelings and emotions can be communicated in a relationship.

VERBAL EXPRESSION OF FEELINGS

Communicating your feelings clearly depends upon your being aware of your feelings, accepting them, and being skillful in their constructive expression. When an individual is unaware or unaccepting of his feelings or unskillful in expressing them, feelings are expressed through

1. *Labeling others.* When a person feels angry, he may label another self-centered and hostile; when he feels warm, he may label another understanding; when he feels embarrassed, he may label another crude.
2. *Commands,* such as "Shut up."
3. *Questions,* such as "Is it safe to drive this fast?"
4. *Accusations,* such as "You don't care about me."
5. *Name-calling,* such as "You're a creep."
6. *Sarcasm,* such as "You certainly make a person feel appreciated!"
7. *Expressions of approval,* such as "You're wonderful."
8. *Expressions of disapproval,* such as "You're terrible."

Although we usually try to describe our ideas clearly and accurately, we rarely try to describe our feelings clearly and accurately. Feelings get expressed in many different ways, but we usually do not attempt to identify and verbally describe the feeling itself. There are at least four ways in which feelings may be described verbally.

1. Identify or name it: "I feel angry," "I feel embarrassed," "I feel warm towards you."
2. Use similes. Because we do not have enough names or labels to describe all our emotions, we invent metaphors to describe our feelings: "I feel stepped on," "I feel squelched," "I feel like a pink cloud floating on air."
3. Report what kind of action the feelings urge you to do: "I feel like hugging you," "I'd like to slap your face," "I wish I could walk over you."
4. Many figures of speech serve as descriptions of feelings, such as, "I feel like God is smiling on me," "I feel like rain continually falls on me."

In describing a feeling you try to make clear what feelings you are experiencing by identifying them. A description of a feeling must be a personal statement, that is, it must refer to "I," "me," or "my," and it must specify some kind of feeling by name, action urge, simile, or some other figure of speech. Any spoken statement can convey feelings. Even the comment, "It's a warm day," can be said so that it expresses resentment or irritation. When we express feelings ambiguously so that the verbal content of the message and the nonverbal cues associated with the message are not in agreement, we confuse the receiver. In order to express feelings constructively so as to build and maintain a close friendship, you must be concerned with the clear and accurate communication of your feelings, especially the feelings of warmth, affection, and caring. Conveying feelings by commands, questions, accusations, or judgments will tend to confuse the person with whom you are building a relationship while the description of your feelings will clearly and accurately communicate what you are feeling. When you want to express your feelings, your ability to describe them is essential for constructive communication.

There are two common results from describing your feelings to another person. First, describing your feelings often helps you to become more aware of what it is you actually do feel. Many times we have feelings that seem ambiguous or unclear to us; getting involved in trying to describe them to another person often clarifies them to ourselves as well as to the other. Second, describing your feelings often begins a dialogue that will improve your relationship with the other person. If another person is to respond to your feelings, he must know what the feelings are. Even if the feelings are negative, it is often productive to express them. Negative feelings are signals that something may be going wrong in the relationship and thus you and the other person need to examine what is going on in your relationship and how your relationship may be improved. By reporting your feelings, you provide information that is necessary if you and the other person are to understand and improve your relationship. When discussing your relationship with another person, a description of your feelings conveys maximum information about what you feel in a way that will probably be more constructive than commands, questions, accusations, and judgments.

Before you proceed, you may wish to check your comprehension of the above material by answering the following questions (answers on p. 101):

1. Name the eight ways in which feelings are expressed without actually describing them.
   a. Shouting.
   b. Labeling others.
   c. Questions.

d. Lecturing.

e. Footnoting.

f. Commands.

g. Accusations.

h. Name-calling.

i. Whispering.

j. Sarcasm.

k. Paraphrasing.

l. Expressions of approval.

m. Expressions of disapproval.

2. What are four ways of describing feelings?

   a. Using feedback techniques.

   b. Identifying the feeling or naming it.

   c. Using value judgments.

   d. Using similes of the feeling.

   e. Using other figures of speech.

   f. Reporting what kind of action the feelings urge you to do.

   g. Painting a picture.

3. What are the two elements of a description of feeling?

   a. A personal statement.

   b. Beginning with "I feel."

   c. Specifying some kind of feeling by name.

   d. Revealing everything you are feeling.

4. What are two common results of expressing your feeling in a relationship?

   a. Getting into a personal argument.

   b. Helping you become more aware of what your feelings really are.

   c. Beginning a dialogue with the other person.

   d. Helping you understand other people.

DESCRIBING YOUR FEELINGS

The objective of this exercise, which has been adapted from an exercise created by John L. Wallen, is to help you recognize when you are displaying your feelings without describing them. For each of the ten items beginning on p. 94 there are two or three statements. One is a description of a feeling; the others are expressions which do not describe the feeling involved. The procedure for the exercise is as follows:

1. Divide into groups of three.

2. For Item One, put a *D* before the sentence that conveys feelings by describing the speaker's feeling. Put a *No* before the sentence that

conveys feeling but does not describe what it is. Mark the answers for Item One only; do not go on to Item Two yet.

3. Compare your answers to Item One with those of the other members of your trio. Discuss the reasons for any differences.

4. Turn to the answers (beginning on p. 95) and read the answers for Item One. Discuss the answers in your trio until you all believe you understand the point being made.

5. Repeat Steps 2, 3, and 4 for Item Two. Then continue the same procedure for each item until you have completed all ten items.

Item 1. (_____) a. Shut your mouth! Don't say another word!

(_____) b. What you just said really annoys me.

Item 2. (_____) a. What's the matter with your eyes? Can't you see I'm trying to work?

(_____) b. I really resent your interrupting me so often.

(_____) c. You don't care about anybody else's feelings. You're completely self-centered.

Item 3. (_____) a. I feel depressed about some things that happened today.

(_____) b. This has been a terrible day.

Item 4. (_____) a. You're such a wonderful person.

(_____) b. I really respect your ideas—you're so well-informed.

Item 5. (_____) a. When I'm around you I feel at ease and free to be myself.

(_____) b. We all feel you're really great.

(_____) c. Everyone likes you.

Item 6. (_____) a. If things don't get better around here, I'm going to find a new job.

(_____) b. Did you ever see such a rotten place to live?

(_____) c. I'm afraid I need help with this exercise.

Item 7. (_____) a. This is a very interesting book.

(_____) b. I feel this is not a very good exercise.

(_____) c. I get very excited when I read this book.

Item 8. (_____) a. I don't feel adequate to contribute anything to this group.

(_____) b. I am not adequate to contribute anything to this group.

Item 9. (_____) a. I am a born loser—I'll never find someone who likes me.

(_____) b. That teacher is terrible—he didn't teach me anything.

(_____) c. I'm depressed because I flunked that test.

Item 10. (_____) a. I feel warm and comfortable in my group.

(_____) b. Someone from my group always seems to be near when I want company.

(_____) c. I feel everyone cares that I'm a part of this group.

ANSWERS TO EXERCISE ON DESCRIBING YOUR FEELINGS

Item 1. a: No   Commands like these exhibit strong emotion but do not name the feeling prompting them.

b: D   Speaker says he feels annoyed.

Item 2. a: No   Questions that express strong feeling without naming it.

b: D   Speaker states he feels resentment.

c: No   Accusation that expresses strong negative feelings. Because the feelings are not named, we do not know whether the accusations originate from anger, disappointment, hurt, or another source.

Item 3. a: D   Speaker says he feels depressed.

b: No   The statement appears to describe what kind of day it was. In fact, it expresses the speaker's negative feelings without saying whether he feels depressed, annoyed, lonely, humiliated, rejected, or whatever.

Item 4. a: No   This value judgment reveals positive feelings about the other person but does not describe what they are. Does the speaker like the other person, respect him, enjoy him, admire him, love him, or what?

b: D   The speaker describes his positive feeling as respect.

Item 5: a: D   A clear description of how the speaker feels when with the other person.

b: No First, the speaker does not speak for himself but hides behind the phrase, "We feel." Second, "You're really great" is a value judgment and does not name a feeling.

c: No The statement does name a feeling ("likes"), but the speaker attributes it to everyone and does not make clear that the feeling is within him. A description of feeling must contain "I," "me," "my," or "mine" to make clear that the feelings are within the speaker. Does it seem more affectionate for a person to tell you, "I like you," or "Everybody likes you"?

Item 6. a: No Conveys negative feelings by talking about the condition of this job. Does not describe the speaker's inner state.

b: No A question that expresses a negative value judgment about the place where he lives. It does not describe what the speaker is feeling.

c: D A clear description of how the speaker feels about this exercise. He feels afraid. Expressions *a* and *b* are criticisms that could come from the kind of fear described in *c*.

Negative criticisms and value judgments often seem like expressions of anger. In fact, negative value judgment and accusations often stem from the speaker's fear, hurt feelings, disappointments, or loneliness.

Item 7. a: No A positive value judgment that conveys positive feelings but does not state what type they are.

b: No Although the person begins by saying, "I feel . . . ," he does not then name what he is feeling. Instead he passes a negative value judgment on the exercise. Note that merely placing the words *I feel* in front of a statement does not make the statement a description of feeling. People often say "I feel" when they mean "I think" or "I believe"; for example, "I feel the Yankees will win," or, "I feel you don't like me."

c: D The speaker describes his feeling when reading this book.

Many times persons who say they are unaware of what they feel—or who say they don't have any feelings about something—state value judgments without recognizing that this is the way their positive or negative feelings get expressed.

Many arguments can be avoided if we were careful to describe our feelings instead of expressing them through value judgments. For example, if Joe says the book is interesting and Fred says it is boring, they may argue about which it "really" is. However, if Joe says he was excited by the book and Fred says he was frustrated by it, no argument should follow. Each person's feelings are what they are. Of course, discussing what it means for each to feel as he does may provide helpful information about each person and about the book itself.

Item 8. a: D Speaker says he feels inadequate.

 b: No Careful! This sounds much the same as the previous statement. However, it says that the speaker actually *is* inadequate—not that he just currently feels this way. The speaker has evaluated himself—has passed a negative value judgment on himself and labeled himself inadequate.

This subtle difference was introduced because many individuals confuse feeling and being. A person may feel inadequate to contribute in a group and yet make helpful contributions. Similarly, he may feel adequate and yet perform very inadequately. A person may feel hopeless about a situation that turns out not to be hopeless.

A sign of emotional maturity may be that a person does not confuse what he feels with the reality of the situation around him. Such a person knows he can perform adequately even though he feels inadequate to the task. He does not let his feelings keep him from doing his best because he knows the difference between feelings and performance and knows that the two do not always match.

Item 9. a: No The speaker has evaluated himself—passed a negative judgment on himself by labeling himself as a born loser.

 b: No Instead of labeling himself a failure, the speaker blames the teacher. This is another value judgment and not a description of a feeling.

 c: D The speaker states he feels depressed. Statements *a* and *c* illustrate the important difference between passing judgment on yourself and describing your feelings.

Feelings can and do change. To say that you are now depressed does not imply that you will or must always feel the same. If you label yourself as a born loser however, or if you truly think of yourself as a born loser, you increase the likelihood that you will act like a born loser. One girl stated this important insight for herself this way, "I have always thought I was a shy person. Many new things I really would have liked to do I avoided—I'd tell myself that I was too shy. Now I have discovered that I am not shy, although at times I *feel* shy."

Many of us try to avoid new things, and thus avoid growing, by label-ing ourselves. "I'm not artistic." "I'm not creative." "I'm not articulate." "I can't speak in groups." If we could recognize what our feelings are beneath such statements, maybe we would be more willing to risk doing things we are somewhat fearful of.

Item 10.　a: D　The speaker says he feels warm and comfortable.

　　　　　b: No　Expresses positive feelings but does not say whether he feels happy, warm, useful, supported, or what.

　　　　　c: No　Instead of "I feel," the speaker should have said, "I believe." The last part of the statement really tells what the speaker believes the *others feel* about him and not what he feels. Expressions *c* and *a* relate to each other as follows: "Because I believe that every-one cares whether I am a part of the group, I feel warm and comfortable."

EXERCISE ON AMBIGUITY OF EXPRESSION OF FEELINGS

The objective of this exercise is to increase your awareness of the am-biguity or unclearness in expressing feelings in ways that are not de-scriptive. Given below are a series of statements. Each statement presents an interpersonal situation. The procedure for the exercise is as follows:

1. Divide into trios.

2. For each situation below write descriptions of two *different* feelings that might have given rise to the expression of feelings in the statement.

3. Compare your answers with the answers of the other members of your trio. Discuss until you understand each other's answers.

4. In the group as a whole, discuss the results of ambiguity in express-ing feelings in interpersonal relationships.
   a. What happens when persons make ambiguous statements of feel-ing? How do other persons respond? How do they feel?
   b. Why would you state feelings ambiguously? In what circumstances would you be ambiguous rather than descriptive? What would be the probable consequence?

1. A girl asks her boy friend, "Why can't you ever be any place on time?" What might the girl have said that would have described her feelings openly?

　　a. _____

　　_____

　　b. _____

　　_____

2. You notice that a person in the group who was talking a lot has suddenly become silent. What might the person have said that would have described his feelings openly?

   a. _____

   _____

   b. _____

   _____

3. During a group meeting, you hear John tell Bill, "Bill, you're talking too much." What might John have said that would have described his feelings openly?

   a. _____

   _____

   b. _____

   _____

4. Sally abruptly changed the subject after Ann made a comment. What might Sally have said that would have described her feelings openly?

   a. _____

   _____

   b. _____

   _____

5. A boy told his girl friend, "You shouldn't have brought me such an expensive gift." What might the boy have said that would have described his feelings openly?

   a. _____

   _____

   b. _____

   _____

6. You hear a passenger say to a taxi-driver, "Do we have to drive this fast?" What might the passenger have said that would have described his feelings openly?

   a. _____

   _____

   b. _____

   _____

7. Sam says to Jane, "You're really wonderful." What might Sam have said that would have described his feelings openly?

a. _____

_____

b. _____

_____

CHECKING YOUR PERCEPTION OF ANOTHER'S FEELINGS

In addition to communicating your feelings to other individuals as clearly and accurately as possible, it is important that you check out your perceptions of other persons' feelings. The reason for this is that perceptions of other persons' feelings are more often the result of what you are feeling, or are afraid of, or are wishing for, than of the other person's verbal, nonverbal, and behavioral cues. If you feel guilty, for example, you may see another person's feelings, and often do, inaccurately. Thus it is important to check them out.

A perception check is used to make sure you understand the feelings of others. Checking perceptions involves describing in a tentative fashion what you perceive as the other person's feelings. It is similar to paraphrasing except that it involves interpreting feelings rather than the words and overt behavior of the other person. Checking perceptions is tentative; it attempts to free the other person so that he wants to describe his own feelings directly. In *checking perceptions* you state what you perceive to be the feeling of the other person. A good perception check conveys the message, "I want to understand your feelings; do you feel . . ." Thus you transform his expressions of feeling into a tentative description of his feeling. The following are examples:

1. "Am I right that you feel disappointed that nobody commented on your suggestion?"
2. "Did you feel angry about what John just said?"
3. "I get the impression that you are annoyed with me. Are you?"
4. "I'm not sure whether your expression means that my remark hurt your feelings, irritated you, or confused you."

Note that a perception check identifies the other person's feelings in some way, and does not express disapproval or approval of the feelings. It merely says, "This is how I perceive your feelings. Am I correct?"

Perception-checking responses aim

1. to communicate that you want to understand the other person as a person—and that means understanding his feelings; and

2. to help you to avoid actions that you later regret because they are based upon false assumptions of what the other person was feeling.

You may wish to answer the following questions (answers on p. 101):

1. What is a perception check?
   a. A statement to check on how you feel.
   b. A statement to check on your perception of the other person's feelings.
   c. A statement to check on the other person's perception of your feelings.
   d. A statement to your bank about your checking account.

2. What are the two aspects of a perception check?
   a. It identifies the other person's feelings.
   b. It identifies your feelings about the other person.
   c. It restates the other person's statements.
   d. It does not express approval or disapproval.

CHECKLIST OF SKILLS

1. I have mastered the following:

   _____ Describing my feelings to others in a direct way.

   _____ Using a perception check when it is needed.

   _____ Avoiding the indirect expression of feelings through commands, questions, accusations, and so on.

2. I need more work on the following:

   _____ Describing my feelings to others in a direct way.

   _____ Using a perception check when it is needed.

   _____ Avoiding the indirect expression of feelings through commands, questions, accusations, and so on.

ANSWERS

Page 89:   1: *b, d, e;* 2: *b, c;* 3: *b;* 4: *c, e, f, g*
Page 93:   1: *b, c, f, g, h, j, l, m;* 2: *b, d, e, f;* 3: *a, c;* 4: *b, c*
Page 101:   1: *b;* 2: *a, d*

The Nonverbal Expression
of Feelings

chapter

6

Although the awareness, acceptance, and expression of feelings is crucial for psychological health and for the building and maintaining of fulfilling relationships, many people have great difficulties in clearly and accurately communicating how they feel to other individuals. Expressing positive feelings such as warmth is a crucial interpersonal skill. In the previous chapter we focused upon the constructive ways of expressing feelings verbally. Like all communication, however, feelings are expressed in nonverbal and behavioral ways as well as verbally. In this chapter we will focus upon the skills necessary for effective nonverbal expression of feelings. The objectives of the chapter are

1. To increase your self-awareness of how you communicate feelings to others.
2. To provide skill practice in expressing feelings nonverbally.
3. To remind you of the importance of the congruence between your verbal, nonverbal, and behavioral cues in clearly and accurately communicating your feelings to another person.

NONVERBAL COMMUNICATION

In communicating effectively with other individuals it may be more important to have a mastery of nonverbal communication than fluency with words. In a normal two-person conversation the verbal components carry less than 35 percent of the social meaning of the situation while more than 65 percent is carried by nonverbal messages (McCroskey, Larson, & Knapp, 1971). This may seem surprising to you, but we communicate by our manner of dress, physique, posture, body tension, facial expressions, degree of eye contact, hand and body movements, tone of voice, continuities in speech (such as rate, duration, nonfluencies and pauses), spatial distance, and touch as well as by words. In order to communicate effectively with other persons, therefore, you must be as concerned with the nonverbal messages you are sending as with the verbal ones, if not more so.

By comparison with verbal language, however, nonverbal behavior is very limited. Usually it is used to communicate feelings, likings, and preferences, and it customarily reinforces or contradicts the feelings that are communicated verbally. A major problem in communicating feelings is that feelings are communicated less by words a person uses than by his nonverbal cues. Particularly important in communicating feelings are facial and vocal cues; smiles, for example, communicate friendliness, cooperativeness, and acceptance to other individuals; there appears to be more eye contact between people who like each other than between people who do not like each other; and emotional meanings are communicated quite accurately through vocal expressions.

It is often difficult to know what another person really feels. He says one thing but does another; he seems to like you but never says so; he says he has great affection for you but somehow you don't feel he is sincere. Feelings are often misunderstood and misinterpreted for two major reasons: one, the ambiguity of nonverbal messages, and the other, the frequent contradictions between verbal and nonverbal messages.

Nonverbal messages are inevitably ambiguous; therefore, the receiver is unclear as to what the sender is feeling. The same feeling can be expressed nonverbally in several different ways; for example, anger may be communicated by great bodily motion or by a frozen stillness. Any single nonverbal cue, furthermore, can arise from a variety of feelings; a blush may indicate embarrassment, pleasure, or even hostility. There are wide differences among social groups as to the meaning of many nonverbal cues; standing close to the receiver may be a sign of warmth to a person from one cultural background and a sign of aggressiveness and hostility to a person from another cultural background. In understanding nonverbal messages, the receiver must interpret the sender's actions and, as these actions increase in ambiguity, the chance for misinterpretation increases.

Correct judgments of the feelings of other individuals are often made difficult by the different degrees of feelings, or contradictory kinds of feelings, being expressed simultaneously through verbal and nonverbal messages. We have all been in situations in which we have received or sent conflicting messages on verbal and nonverbal channels. The parent who screams, "I WANT IT QUIET AROUND THIS HOUSE," or the teacher who says, "I've always got plenty of time to talk to a student" while he glances at his watch and nervously begins packing his briefcase, are examples. Sometimes a person may say, "I like you," but communicate nonverbally by a cold tone of voice, looking worried, and backing away, "Don't come close to me." When receiving such conflicting messages through two different channels, we tend to believe the message that we perceive to be harder to fake. This is often the nonverbal channel. You are, therefore, more apt to believe the nonverbal communication than the verbal one. Such contradictory communications are known as "double binds" and can cause anxiety and suspiciousness in the receiver.

Nonverbal messages, in summary, are more powerful in communicating feelings than are verbal messages, but also more ambiguous and different to interpret accurately. To communicate your feelings clearly and accurately to another person, you need to be skillful in both the verbal and nonverbal ways of expressing feelings. Above all, you need to make your verbal and nonverbal messages congruent with each other. The following exercises will help you become more aware of the ambiguity of nonverbal messages, more aware of how you presently communicate feelings nonverbally, and will help you become more skillful in the use of nonverbal cues to communicate feelings.

You may wish to test your understanding of this section by answering the following questions (answers on p. 115):

1. Which carries more of the social meaning of a situation?
   a. Verbal messages.
   b. Nonverbal messages.

2. Which type of message is usually more ambiguous?
   a. Verbal.
   b. Nonverbal.

3. Which type of channel can include a greater variety and complexity of messages?
   a. Verbal.
   b. Nonverbal.

4. The sources of ambiguity in nonverbal messages are that:
   a. The same feeling can be expressed several different ways.
   b. The sender has had too much to drink.
   c. Any single nonverbal cue can arise from a variety of feelings.
   d. They do not include words.
   e. Among different social groups there are wide differences in the meaning of nonverbal cues.

5. A situation in which contradictory messages are sent over the verbal and nonverbal channels of communication is known as:
   a. A double message.
   b. A double bind.
   c. A mixup.
   d. An accident.

EXERCISE ON COMMUNICATION WITHOUT WORDS

The objective of this exercise, adapted from one developed by John Wallen, is to increase your awareness of the ambiguity of expressing feelings in nonverbal or in behavioral ways. Given below are a series of situations. Each involves the expression of feelings through certain nonverbal behaviors. The procedure for the exercise is as follows:

1. Divide into groups of three.

2. For each situation describe two different feelings (within the person named) that might have given rise to such a nonverbal expression of feelings.

3. Compare your answers with the answers of the other members of your trio. Discuss until you understand each other's answers.

4. In the group as a whole, share your feelings and reactions to the exercise. What did you learn? How would you react if someone in the group behaved similarly to the people in the situations described? Are there any times when the nonverbal expression of feelings is more effective than the verbal description of feelings?

1. Nancy, who had been talking a lot in the group, suddenly became silent. Describe two feelings that might have caused Nancy to do this.

   a. _____

   b. _____

2. Without expression, Lucy suddenly changed the subject of the group's discussion. What are two different feelings that might have been responsible for Lucy's changing the subject?

   a. _____

   b. _____

3. Whenever George made a comment in the group, he watched the leader's face. What are two different feelings that might have led George to watch the leader so intently?

   a. _____

   b. _____

4. While the group discussion was going on, Betty became more and more tense and restless. Finally, she got up abruptly and left the room without saying a word. Describe two different feelings that might have caused Betty to leave.

    a. _____

    b. _____

5. Ron was describing seriously a fight he and a friend had had earlier. In the middle of his discussion, John began to laugh. Describe two different feelings that might have caused John to laugh.

    a. _____

    b. _____

INTERPRETING OTHERS' NONVERBAL CUES

The objectives of this exercise are (1) to demonstrate the ambiguity of nonverbal cues in communicating feelings and (2) to illustrate how many different feeling reactions the same nonverbal cues can give. For this exercise you need from five to ten pictures cut out of magazines. Each picture should have at least one person in it who is expressing a feeling. The procedure for the exercise is as follows:

1. Number the pictures. Pass each picture around the group.
2. Each person answers the following questions about each picture:
    a. How do the individuals in the picture feel?
    b. How does this picture make you feel?
3. The group then share their answers for each picture.
    a. How similar were your interpretations of what the individuals in the pictures felt?
    b. How similar were the feelings you had in response to the pictures?
    c. What makes the pictures so ambiguous (if you found that you did give dissimilar answers)?
    d. Could different people interpret your own nonverbal cues as many different ways as the group interpreted the nonverbal cues of the individuals in the pictures?

HOW DO YOU EXPRESS YOUR FEELINGS?

The objective of this exercise, adapted from one developed by John Wallen, is to increase your self-awareness of the ways in which you express your feelings. Given below are a series of feelings you may have experienced. For each of these you are to report two different ways that you express such feelings. The first answer should be something you would say that would express your feelings. The second answer should report how you might express such feelings by actions and without using words. The procedure for the exercise is as follows:

1. Divide into groups of three.
2. Write out your answers to the situations following.
3. Compare your answers with the answers of the other members of your trio. Discuss until you understand each other's answers. Then discuss:
   a. What did I learn about the way I usually express my feelings?
   b. In what ways would it be helpful for me to change the ways in which I usually express my feelings?
   c. In what ways would it be helpful for each of you to change the ways in which you usually express feelings?
4. In the group as a whole, share your feelings and reactions to the exercise. Then list as many principles for constructively expressing feelings as you can think of:

   a. _____
   b. _____
   c. _____
   d. _____
   e. _____
   f. _____

1. When you feel bored with what is going on in a discussion, how do you usually express your feeling?

   Using words: _____

   Without using words: _____

2. When you feel very annoyed with another person with whom you want to build a better relationship, how do you usually express your feeling?

   Using words: _____

   Without using words: _____

3. When another person says or does something to you that hurts your feelings deeply, how do you usually express your feeling?

   Using words: _____

   Without using words: _____

4. An acquaintance asks you to do something that you are afraid you cannot do well. You also want to hide the fact that you feel inadequate. How do you express your feelings?

Using words: _____

Without using words: _____

5. You feel affection and fondness for someone else but at the same time can't be sure the other person feels the same way about you. How do you usually express your feelings?

Using words: _____

Without using words: _____

6. Your close friend is leaving town for a long time and you feel alone and lonely. How would you usually express your feelings?

Using words: _____

Without using words: _____

THE USE OF NONVERBAL CUES TO EXPRESS WARMTH AND COLDNESS

The objective of this exercise is to increase your skills in the use of non-verbal cues to express warmth. In order to increase your awareness of which nonverbal cues express warmth, you will be asked to role play the expression of coldness as well as the expression of warmth. Some of the nonverbal cues which indicate warmth or coldness are:

Nonverbal Cue	Warmth	Coldness
Tone of Voice	soft	hard
Facial Expression	smiling, interested	poker-faced, frowning, disinterested
Posture	lean toward other; relaxed	lean away from other; tense
Eye Contact	look into other's eyes	avoid looking into other's eyes
Touching	touch other softly	avoid touching other
Gestures	open, welcoming	closed, guarding oneself and keeping other away
Spatial Distance	close	distant

The procedure for the exercise is as follows:

1. Divide into pairs. Designate one person *A* and the other *B*.
2. Person *A* makes three statements about his childhood in a warm way. Then Person *A* makes three statements about his childhood in a cold way.
3. Person *B* gives Person *A* feedback on how successfully he role played the nonverbal expression of warmth and coldness.
4. Reverse roles and repeat steps 2 and 3.
5. Find a new partner. Repeat steps 2 and 3 with your new partner. This time discuss the characteristics of a person you want as a friend.
6. Find a new partner. Repeat steps 2 and 3 with your new partner. This time discuss what you could do to improve your relationship with your partner.
7. Discuss the exercise in the group as a whole.
   a. Did you find it easy to role play warmth and coldness? Why or why not?
   b. How well did each of you master the skills of expressing warmth and coldness nonverbally?
   c. Are there other ways to express warmth nonverbally?
   d. What were your reactions and feelings to the exercise?
8. Go around the group and give each other feedback concerning the typical nonverbal messages you send in the group. How would you describe each other's nonverbal behavior? What is most distinctive about each person's nonverbal behavior? If you were to suggest one way for each person to change his nonverbal behavior, what would it be?

Expressing warmth is a vital skill for building and maintaining fulfilling relationships. More than any other behavior, warmth communicates liking, concern, and acceptance of another person. You should practice the nonverbal expression of warmth until you are sure that you can effectively communicate it when you want it.

A CARD GAME FOR PRACTICING NONVERBAL COMMUNICATION

The following game involves the nonverbal expression of feelings. Sit on the floor in a circle. Do not use a table. Deal out a deck of ordinary playing cards until everyone has the same number of cards and there are at least three cards left in a draw-deck. The draw-deck is placed face down in the center of the circle. The first person to get rid of all his cards is the *winner*. You get rid of your cards by correctly identifying the emotions expressed by other players and by accurately communicating emotions to the other players. In the game you take turns expressing one emotion. To begin the player on the dealer's left selects a card from his own hand and lays it face down in front of him. He is now the expresser; the remaining players are to correctly identify the emotion he expresses. He then expresses the feeling represented by the card (see below). The other players check their hands to see if they have a card that matches the emotion that was expressed. If so, they place the card (or cards) face down in front of them. If not, they pass. When all the cards are down for the first round, they are all turned face up at once. If one or more of the receivers have matched the expresser's card, the expresser puts his card and all the matching cards face down on the bottom of the draw-deck. Any of the players who put down a wrong card must return it to their hand and draw an additional card from the top of the draw-deck. You draw the same number of cards from the draw-deck that you put down in front of you. If no other player, however, matched the expresser's card, then the expresser failed to communicate; he returns his card to his hand and draws a penalty card from the draw-deck. In this case the receivers return their cards to their hands but *do not* draw penalty cards.

When you hold two or three cards of the same emotion, you must play all the cards if you play one of them. As expresser or receiver, you may get rid of two or three cards, or you may have to draw two or three penalty cards.

The expresser may use any nonverbal behavior he wishes to in order to communicate accurately the emotion he is portraying, except the use of vocal cues. No words may be spoken. You may wish to use your hands, your head, your whole body, and you may involve other players by touching them or engaging them in a nonverbal interchange.

Each card represents a different emotion. The emotions the cards represent are as follows:

2	= contentment	9	= anger
3	= shyness	10	= hope
4	= indifference	Jack	= happiness
5	= fear	Queen	= joy
6	= frustration	King	= warmth
7	= loneliness	Ace	= love
8	= sorrow		

RECOGNIZING CUES FOR AFFECTION OR HOSTILITY

The following exercise is aimed at providing you with an opportunity to see if you can tell the difference between messages indicating affection and messages indicating hostility. Listed below are 38 messages. In the space provided, write an *A* if you think the message indicates affection and an *H* if you think the message indicates hostility. Then check your answers with the answers found on p. 115. Review any that you missed until you are sure you understand it.

_____ 1. Looks directly at the other person; gives his undivided attention.

_____ 2. Offers a cigarette, cup of coffee, or other favor.

_____ 3. Greets the other person (if at all) in a cold, formal manner (refuses to shake hands, does not use other person's name, and so on).

_____ 4. Engages in friendly humor (e.g., self-directed humor or humor facetiously directed at the other person).

_____ 5. Glares at the other person.

_____ 6. Speaks in a harsh tone of voice.

_____ 7. Uses the other person's first name.

_____ 8. Physically abuses the other person (hits, shoves).

_____ 9. Yawns or shows other signs of boredom.

_____ 10. Seems at ease; has a relaxed posture; does not appear tense or exhibit nervous mannerisms.

_____ 11. Deprecates the other person's statements, accomplishments, background, home town, alma mater, and so forth.

_____ 12. Lays verbal traps for the other person (e.g., "Just a minute ago you said [in response to leading] . . . Now you're contradicting yourself.")

_____ 13. Smiles an expression of cordiality.

_____ 14. Sits close to the other person.

_____ 15. Interrupts repeatedly.

_____ 16. Leans towards the other person as an expression of interest.

_____ 17. Makes casual physical contact with the other person as an expression of affection (e.g., friendly slap on the back, rap on the arm).

_____ 18. Shows consideration for the physical comfort of the other person (e.g., takes person's coat, offers more comfortable chair, adjusts window, asks permission before smoking).

_____ 19. Sits relatively far away.

_____ 20. Reduces the other person's remarks to the absurd.

_____ 21. Confides "personal" information to the other person.

_____ 22. Attempts to "snow" the other person by using overly intellectual or otherwise unfamiliar vocabulary.

_____ 23. Makes biting, sarcastic remarks about the other person.

_____ 24. Makes encouraging, reassuring remarks to the other person.

_____ 25. Uses ad hominems (e.g., "That stupid remark is about what I would expect from someone like you.").

_____ 26. Ignores the other person (by looking away from him, looking out the window, glancing repeatedly at watch, busying self with papers on desk).

_____ 27. Praises or compliments something the other person has said or done.

_____ 28. Expresses an interest in seeing and talking again with the other person.

_____ 29. Uses the "lingo" of the other person.

_____ 30. Exhibits an open and receptive facial expression.

_____ 31. Mocks or teases the other person.

_____ 32. Extends a cordial greeting to the other person.

_____ 33. Smiles when the other person makes a humorous remark.

_____ 34. Exhibits a cold, nonreceptive facial expression (e.g., set jaw; noninvolved, blank look).

_____ 35. Talks enthusiastically about the other person's hobbies or interests.

_____ 36. States his sympathy for the other person.

_____ 37. Rebuffs or hedges when asked a "personal" question; does not risk interpersonal involvement.

_____ 38. Responds directly and openly to the other person's request to know his opinion, value, attitude, or feeling.

THE IMPORTANCE OF CONGRUENCE AMONG VERBAL, NONVERBAL, AND BEHAVIORAL CUES IN COMMUNICATING FEELINGS

There is no way to emphasize too much the importance of making congruent your verbal, nonverbal, and behavioral messages for communicating feelings. If you wish to express warmth, your words, your facial expression, tone of voice, posture, and so on, and your behavior must all communicate warmth. Contradictory messages will only indicate to the other person that you are untrustworthy and will make him anxious about his relationship with you. Some psychologists have stated that receiving contradictory verbal and nonverbal messages for a long period of time from someone you love can result in mental illness. For a person to believe your expression of feelings is real and genuine, the verbal, nonverbal, and behavioral messages must be congruent. This is as true of feelings such as anger as it is of feelings such as warmth.

CHECKLIST OF SKILLS

1. Indicate below the skills you have mastered:

_____ Using nonverbal cues to express feelings.

_____ Being aware of how I express my feelings nonverbally.

_____ Being congruent in the way my verbal, nonverbal, and behavioral messages express feelings.

_____ Using nonverbal cues to express warmth.

2. I need more work on:

_____ Using nonverbal cues to express feelings.

_____ Being aware of how I express my feelings nonverbally.

_____ Being congruent in the way my verbal, nonverbal, and behavioral messages express feelings.

_____ Using nonverbal cues to express warmth.

ANSWERS

Pages 105–106:   1: b; 2: b; 3: a; 4: a, c, e; 5: b

Pages 112–114—Recognizing Cues for Affection or Hostility: 1: A; 2: A; 3: H; 4: A; 5: H; 6: H; 7: A; 8: H; 9: H; 10: A; 11: H; 12: H; 13: A; 14: A; 15: H; 16: A; 17: A; 18: A; 19: H; 20: H; 21: A; 22: H; 23: H; 24: A; 25: H; 26: H; 27: A; 28: A; 29: A; 30: A; 31: H; 32: A; 33: A; 34: H; 35: A; 36: A; 37: H; 38: A

Helpful Styles of Listening and Responding

How do you respond to another person's problems and concerns? When someone is talking about something deeply distressing or of real concern to him, how should you respond to be helpful? How do you answer in ways which will both help the person solve his problem or clarify his feelings and at the same time help build a closer relationship between that person and yourself?

RESPONDING TO ANOTHER'S PROBLEMS

Perhaps the most important thing to remember is that you cannot solve someone else's problems for him. No matter how sure you are of what the right thing to do is or how much insight you think you have into another person's problems, the other person must come to his own decisions about what he should do and achieve his own insights into the situation and himself. So how do you respond to make sure that the person will come to his own decision and gain his own insights?

In responding to another person's messages, there are two basic aspects which determine the effectiveness of the response: (1) the intentions of the receiver as he gives his response, and (2) the actual phrasing of the response itself. The exercises which follow will deal with both aspects. Of the two elements of a response, intent and phrasing, the receiver's intentions are the most important single factor in influencing the sender's ability to solve his problem. In order to examine the attitudes with which a person can respond to someone asking for help with a problem or a concern we will go through the following exercise.

In order to determine how well you understood the material in this section, please answer the following questions (answers on p. 139):

1. What is the most important thing to remember about helping another person with his problems and concerns?
   a. You can solve his problems for him.
   b. You cannot solve his problems for him.
   c. He can help you solve your problems.
   d. He may not have any problems.

2. What are the two basic aspects of a response which influence its effectiveness?
   a. The attitude of the receiver as he delivers his response.
   b. The attitude of the receiver as he gossips later with a friend about the conversation.
   c. The actual wording of the response itself.
   d. The responses the receiver doesn't choose to give out of all the possible responses he could give.

EXERCISE ON LISTENING AND RESPONSE STYLES

The objectives of this exercise are (1) for you to identify your response style, (2) to provide you with an understanding of the different types of responses available in a situation where the sender has a problem he wants help with, and (3) for you to examine when each type of response may be most effective in helping the person with his problem and in building a closer relationship. The general procedure for the exercise is as follows:

1. Each person answers the "Questionnaire on Listening and Response Styles." The specific instructions are on "Answer Sheet I," p. 247.
2. Identify the underlying intent of each response given in the questionnaire. The specific instructions are on "Answer Sheet II," p. 249.
3. Using the scoring key on page 251, score "Answer Sheet I." Indicate the number of times you used each type of response in the appropriate space on the answer sheet.
4. Divide into groups of three and score "Answer Sheet II," discussing each response until everyone understands it.
5. On Table 7.1 (p. 125), mark the frequency with which each member of the group used each type of response.

6. Use the questions given on pages 125–126 to discuss the results summarized in Table 7.1.

QUESTIONNAIRE ON LISTENING AND RESPONSE STYLES

In this exercise [1] a series of statements is presented. Each statement is an expression by a person about an aspect of the situation he faces. Little or no information is given you about the nature of the person speaking. Following each statement is a series of five possible responses. You are to follow the directions on "Answer Sheet I" concerning the statements and the responses.

1. *Girl*—"I tell you I hate my father. I hate him! I hate him! I hate him! And there's no reason for it. He is a minister—a good and righteous man. He has never laid a hand on me—but I have this terrific feeling against him—and it makes me feel so terrible because—there is no reason for it. It's a sin to hate your father—especially if you don't have any real reason for it. I . . . it worries me."

1. I don't blame you for feeling guilty about hating him, especially since you can't figure out what he has done to make you hate him. And then, too, even though you see only your hatred of him, I bet that underneath it you have some love for him, and this plays a part in your feelings of guilt.
2. Awhile ago I felt the same way, but I hated my mother. I guess lots of kids do. I just avoided her for awhile until things settled down, and things are fine now.
3. That's really strange that you feel that way. You should get things straightened out. A good relationship with your father is a great thing.
4. You're worried that you hate your father without reason and yet feel sinful for hating him.
5. What's your father like? You say he's never hit you, but maybe he has *not* let you do a number of things *you* wanted to do. What do you think?

2. *Boy*—"I have the queerest feeling. Whenever anything good happens to me—I just can't believe it. I act as though it never happened. And it worries me. I wanted a date with Myrtle—and I stood around for weeks before I got up enough courage to ask her for a date, and she said 'yes'—

[1] Adapted from E. H. Porter, Jr., *Therapeutic Counseling* (Boston: Houghton Mifflin Company, 1950), pp. 10–24.

and I couldn't believe it. I couldn't believe it so much that I didn't keep the date."

1. You've got to get with it and get a more realistic idea about women. They're human, too, you know, and want dates just as much as you do.
2. It just doesn't seem real when something good happens to you?
3. You have probably denied to yourself so strongly that anything good could happen to you that when it does it seems unreal.
4. Maybe these feelings of unreality are connected with a particular area of your life. What do you mean when you say, "Whenever anything good happens to me?"
5. It's not a big thing. Lots of people get the same kinds of feelings. You'll snap out of it.

3. *Boy*—"I'm determined to get good grades. I am not afraid of hard work. I am not afraid to take a few hard knocks, if I can see my goal out there in front. And I'm not averse to climbing over a few people who get in my way because this means a lot to me. I can't be satisfied with just mediocre grades. No, I want to *be* somebody."

1. You see yourself as a really ambitious person, is that it?
2. You just have to be out on top, no matter what you may do to others.
3. Why do you feel that it's so important to get good grades?
4. Why don't you take some tests to determine what courses you'd do best in? It might be a big help to you, although I bet that with your drive you could do well in most fields.
5. Determination can be a real asset to anyone. Are you really sure, though, that you mean it when you say you're not against climbing over those who get in your way? Couldn't that be a problem?

4. *Girl*—"I'm afraid to be alone. I really am. I'm afraid I'll kill myself, and I don't want to, but I get so depressed. I get caught in a terrific clutch of fear—it's unreal, but it's there. And I get so anxious I could scream. I want to get outside and I'm afraid to go out in case I run in front of a car—and I'm afraid to stay in—I'm afraid of myself—I'm afraid to go to the doctor to get an examination. I'm afraid he'll tell me it's cancer. My mother had it. My grandmother, my aunt. I've lived with it all my life, and it's hell. And when this first came up . . . see, I break out in a sweat just talking about it. I just can't talk to my father. God, is there any help!"

1. Aside from your fear, have you any symptoms of cancer?

2. This terrific fear just never lets you alone.

3. If you have any reason at all to think that you might have cancer, you really should try to control your fear enough to have a medical examination. It's stupid to worry if there's no reason, and you shouldn't waste time if you do have cancer.

4. Whenever you get that scared, why don't you call me? I'm not saying that I'll be of any help, but maybe you'll feel better if you talk to someone.

5. You feel that you might have cancer because so many people in your family had it, and you're letting that fear creep into every aspect of your life.

5. *Girl*—"I've lived in this town all my life, and in the same house for seven years, but I don't know anybody. At school I just can't seem to make friends. I try to be nice to the other kids, but I feel all uncomfortable inside. And then I tell myself that I don't care. People aren't dependable, everyone is out for himself, I don't want any friends. And sometimes I think I really mean it."

1. Listen, here's what we can do. You can join this club I belong to. Our group is small and we want more members. We go horseback riding and things like that, so even if you are too afraid to make friends at first, at least you can have fun.

2. When you first meet someone, how do you act? What do you say to them?

3. It's gone on so long it almost has you convinced. Is that right?

4. Maybe your not wanting friends is just to cover up for something else.

5. It's pretty hard to be without friends. *I* would really work on that. There are lots of things that you could do to learn how to make friends, and the sooner you start, the better.

6. *Boy (veteran)*—"What's the use of anything? No one plays fair and square with a guy. The fellows who stay at home get all the breaks. They all take advantage of us while we sweat it out at the front. I hate their guts—every one of them. They are all double-crossers. And my girl . . ." (long pause).

1. You started to say something about your girl?

2. You feel they took advantage of you and it really makes you angry.

3. Maybe you resent the guys who stayed home because you are jealous. You wish that you could have stayed home, too.

4. I understand how you feel about that, but it's going to keep you from getting anywhere if you don't try to get away from it.

5. Lots of other people are angry too—sometimes with good reason. But you'll forget it as time goes on and you get things going again.

7. *Boy*—"I tell you I am in one hell of a fix! I'm in love with a really great girl—and she loves me. I'm sure of that. But I'm not good enough for her. I can't ask her to marry me. I've got a criminal record. She doesn't know about it, but I know it'll come out some day. No. I couldn't marry and have children. I've got a record and that proves to the world that I'm no good."

1. Well, it would be unfair to her to marry and to discover about your past later. You have to tell her about it now.

2. You feel afraid to face her with your record because she might break up with you and you just couldn't stand that.

3. Why are you so sure that she wouldn't be able to accept you if she knew about your past?

4. Possibly if you could have her talk to a friend, maybe they could lead her to see that your past is your past and does not necessarily mean that you couldn't have a happy future together.

5. You see yourself as not good enough for her without a doubt?

8. *Girl (physically handicapped)*—"I can't do any of the things my sister does. I can't dance or go riding or date the boys. I'm a . . . I look at Charlene, and I wish I were her. You can't know the feeling I get deep inside me. I want to be able to have pretty clothes like hers, and to go out and have a good time. It makes me sick inside. But she can't help it, she was born that way. And I can't help it because I was born this way . . . and I get this feeling. I *love* my sister, really I do. But I just cry and cry until I am sick. I want the things other girls have. I can't help it—I'm only human. I know it's a sin to feel as I do—but she has everything and I have nothing."

1. Since you realize that you aren't going to be able to do many of the things your sister does, aren't there some other things you'd like to do?

2. I can see why you'd envy her, but since you can't compete with her it's not much use in using up your energy with envy. You've got to settle down and build your own life.

3. In other words, you are jealous of your sister because you can't com-

pete with her and you feel guilty about your envy because you love your sister, too.

4. How do you react to her directly and how does she react to you in some of these situations?

5. You say in one breath that you envy your sister. You say next that you love her. Your feelings of guilt could be due to these contradictory feelings.

9. *Boy*—"I got out of school last month and I thought, 'Now what?' I looked for a job, and right there I ran into a snag. I couldn't make up my mind what to do. I thought I ought to go to college, or I thought I'd be happier if I joined the Navy, and then I looked for a job and nothing stood out as a clear choice. Everything looked bad, and I felt . . . well, what's the use? Am I going crazy? Am I always going to be so messed up inside that I won't be able to move in any direction?"

1. You're wondering what it's all about?

2. Why don't you want them and why do you want them—maybe there's a clue that will help you out.

3. This is one thing many of us have faced. It will disappear in time. Why not just take anything until you get things clear in your mind?

4. You don't need to remain messed up, or you may not be messed up now. You're confused, yes, but if you set your mind to it, I bet you'll overcome your confusion and move ahead all right.

5. You're confused—and upset about it. This can happen, I guess, when we suddenly find ourselves having to make decisions after a long time in high school where even minor decisions were made for us.

10. *Girl*—"Oh, I couldn't work through my problem without help. You ask me questions and tell me . . . because I wouldn't be able to . . . honestly . . . I haven't got any idea how to go about it. I don't want to . . . it's like at school, I can't go ahead on my own, I just can't. I want to be told—then it's not my fault if things go wrong. And they would go wrong, because I don't know how things should be done, I feel so helpless."

1. What do you mean when you say "It's not my fault if things go wrong even after I've been told what to do?"

2. You feel that you just can't do things without help?

3. It's not really that you can't go ahead on your own—it's just that you think you can't. You need to build up your self-confidence.

4. We can talk and then maybe you'll get some ideas to think about and try which may make your school work easier.

5. You feel dependent upon someone else for nearly everything you do, don't you? And it probably scares you when people throw you on your own. But when people tell you what to do you don't have to assume the real responsibility and then it's not your fault if things go wrong—they just didn't tell you enough.

11. *Boy*—"Well this new kid came into class. He's a big shot—has all the answers. Thinks he's going places. But he doesn't know George P. Quipenque! I'll get ahead of him."

1. You feel that you must be out in front. That it is really important to you to be the better man.

2. It's a fine thing to try to get ahead, but by starting out with such an attitude toward him you're going at it all wrong.

3. Boy, that will probably take a lot of hard work and studying. You'll want to go carefully.

4. He really makes you want to beat him out?

5. Hold it. Why is it so important to you to want to get ahead of him?

12. *Boy*—"I've gone steady four times and each time I've thought, 'Boy, this is the real thing!' But none of them has ever been like *this* girl. She's the most beautiful girl you ever saw—and dance! And she dresses like a million dollars. She's out of this world!"

1. You're *really* enthusiastic about her, aren't you?

2. How does she compare with your other girls? How did you feel about them before you went steady?

3. If she's anything like you seem to feel she is, she must be quite a catch. Maybe this time you'll stick.

4. It seems to me kind of odd that every time you've felt the same way.

5. Just stop and listen to what you've said. The reasons that you give for really digging this girl are rather superficial.

INTENTIONS UNDERLYING THE RESPONSES

In exploring the intentions underlying the responses in the preceding questionnaire, we will refer to the person with the problem as the "sender" and the person giving the responses as the "receiver." There are five underlying intentions:

Evaluative (E): a response that indicates the receiver has made a judgment of relative goodness, appropriateness, effectiveness, or rightness of the sender's problem. The receiver has in some way implied what the sender might or ought to do.

Interpretative (I): a response that indicates the receiver's intent is to teach, to tell the sender what his problem means, how the sender really feels about the situation. The receiver has either obviously or subtly implied what the person with the problem might or ought to think.

Supportive (S): a response that indicates the receiver's intent is to reassure, to pacify, to reduce the sender's intensity of feeling. The receiver has in some way implied that the sender need not feel as he does.

Probing (P): a response that indicates the receiver's intent is to seek further information, provoke further discussion along a certain line, question the sender. The receiver has in some way implied that the sender ought or might profitably develop or discuss a point further

Understanding (U): a response that indicates the receiver's intent is to respond only to ask the sender whether the receiver correctly understands what the sender is saying, how the sender feels about the problem, and how the sender sees the problem. This is the same as the paraphrasing response discussed in Chapter 4.

TABLE 7.1   FREQUENCY WITH WHICH THE GROUP
MEMBERS USED EACH TYPE OF RESPONSE

Frequency of Response	*Response Styles*				
	E	I	S	P	U
0–2	____	____	____	____	____
3–5	____	____	____	____	____
6–8	____	____	____	____	____
9–12	____	____	____	____	____

After you have finished the procedure for scoring both answer sheets, mark the frequency with which each member of the group used each type of response. In the group, discuss the results summarized in Table 7.1 and the consequences of each response style. The following questions may be helpful:

1. What were the most frequently used responses by the members of the group?

2. How frequently did you use each of the response styles?

3. When would you want a friend to use each of the different responses in talking with you about your problems and concerns?

4. When is each type of response most useful in helping another person with his problems and concerns and in building a relationship with him?

5. What responses tell the most about the receiver?

PRACTICING THE FIVE RESPONSES

The following exercise provides you with an opportunity to practice each of the five types of responses. The exercise consists of two parts, one in which you are given a problem statement and you write down what you would say (assuming you wanted to respond with each of the five types of intentions), and one in which you and another person make statements and practice with each other giving the different types of responses. The procedure for the exercise is as follows:

1. Read the following paragraphs and write a response for each category. Do this by yourself.

"Sometimes I get so depressed I can hardly stand it. Here I am, 25 years old and still not married. It's not as if I haven't had any chances, but I've never really wanted to marry any of the guys I've dated. All my friends are married; I can't understand why I'm not. Is there something wrong with me?"

Evaluative Response: _____

_____

_____

_____

Interpretative Response: _____

_____

_____

_____

Supportive Response: _____

_____

Probing Response: _____

Understanding Response: _____

"I'm really concerned about a friend of mine named Jane. She never seems to take life seriously enough. She's dropped out of school, she gets a job, and then she quits after a week, she is using drugs and plans to move to a commune. I'm really worried that someday she'll ruin her life. I don't know what I should do."

Evaluative Response: _____

Interpretative Response: _____

Supportive Response: _____

Probing Response: _____

Understanding Response: _____

_____

_____

_____

"I need your advice about my relationship with June. She wants us to get very serious. But I don't even know if I like her. We spend a lot of time together, I have fun when I'm around her, but she's all the time pushing me not to date other girls and to see her more often than I now do. I don't like to be pushed; but I don't want to hurt her by not dating her anymore. What would you do?"

Evaluative Response: _____

_____

_____

_____

Interpretative Response: _____

_____

_____

_____

Supportive Response: _____

_____

_____

_____

Probing Response: _____

_____

_____

_____

Understanding Response: _____

_____

_____

_____

2. Divide into pairs. Discuss each other's answers and make suggestions as to how they might be improved.

3. Think of a problem you now are having either at your job or in school. It may be a major problem or it may be a minor one. Each person in the pairs tell the other his problem. The receiver then gives an evaluative response, an interpretative response, a supportive response, a probing response, and then an understanding response.

4. Think of a problem you are having with your family. It may be either a minor or a major problem. Each person in the pairs tell the other his problem. The receiver gives each of the five responses.

5. Think of a problem, either a major or a minor one, you are having with a friend. Each person in the pairs tell the other his problem. The receiver gives each of the five responses.

6. In the pairs, give each other feedback concerning how well each of you can respond in the five ways discussed in this chapter. You may wish to continue practicing the different responses until you have mastered them to your satisfaction. This can be done by consciously applying them to your everyday conversations or by pairing up with a member of your group and setting specific practice times for the two of you to increase your response skills.

LISTENING AND RESPONDING STYLES

This exercise is based on the work of Carl Rogers, a noted psychologist. Several years ago he conducted a series of studies on how individuals communicate with each other in face-to-face situations. He found that the categories of evaluative, interpretative, supportive, probing, and understanding statements encompass 80 percent of all the messages sent between individuals. The other 20 percent of the statements are incidental and of no real importance. From his observations of individuals in all sorts of different settings, such as businessmen, housewives, parties, conventions, and so on, he found that the responses were used by individuals in the following frequency: (1) evaluative was most used, (2) interpretative was next, (3) supportive was the third most common response, (4) probing the fourth, and (5) understanding the least. Finally, he found that if a person uses one category of response as much as 40 percent of the time, then other people see him as *always* responding that way. This is a process of oversimplification similar to stereotyping.

The categories of response are in themselves neither good nor bad. It is the overuse or underuse of any of the categories that may not be functional or the failure to recognize when each type of response is appropriate that interferes with helping the sender and building a better friendship. If, in answering the above questionnaire, you have used only one or two of the responses, you may overuse some types of responses while you underuse others. This can be easily remedied by becoming more aware of your responses and working to become proficient in using all five types of responses when they seem appropriate.

When is each response appropriate? From your own experience and from listening to the discussion of your group you may have some good ideas. In terms of what is appropriate in the early stage of forming a friendship, two of the possible responses to be most sensitive to are the understanding and the evaluative responses. Basically, the understanding response revolves around the notion that when an individual expresses a message and that message is paraphrased in fresh words with no change in its essential meaning, the sender will expand upon or further explore the ideas, feelings, and attitudes contained in the message, achieve a recognition of previously denied meanings or feelings, or move on to express a new message that is more meaningful to him. Even when the receiver has misunderstood and communicated a faulty understanding of the sender's ideas and feelings, the sender will respond in ways that will clarify the receiver's incorrect response, thus increasing the accuracy and clarity of communication between the two individuals.

It is the understanding response that is most likely to communicate to the sender that the listener is interested in the sender as a person, has an accurate understanding of the sender and of what he is saying, and is most encouraging to the sender to go on and elaborate and further explore his problem. The understanding response may also be the most helpful for enabling the receiver to see the sender's problem from the sender's point of view. Many relationships or conversations are best begun by using the understanding response until a trust level is established; then the other categories of response can be more freely used. The procedures for engaging in the understanding response are rather simple (see Chapter 4), and anyone who takes the time and effort can become quite skillful in their use.

As has been discussed in Chapter 4, the major barrier to mutual understanding is the very natural tendency to judge, evaluate, approve, or disapprove of the messages of the sender. For this reason you should usually avoid giving evaluative responses in the early stages of a relationship or of a conversation about the sender's problems. The primary reaction to a value judgment is another value judgment (for example, "you say I'm wrong, but I think I'm right and you're wrong"), with each person looking at the issue only from his own point of view. This tendency to make evaluations is very much heightened in situations where feelings and emotions are deeply involved, such as when you are discussing a personal problem. Defensiveness and feelings of being threatened are avoided when the listener responds with understanding rather than with evaluative responses. Evaluative responses, however, may be helpful when you are specifically asked to make a value judgment or when you wish to disclose your own values and attitudes.

There will be times when another person tries to discuss an issue with you that you do not understand. Probing responses to get a clear definition of the problem before you respond may be helpful at that time. They may also be helpful if you do not think the sender is seeing the full implications of some of his statements. Supportive responses are useful when the person needs to feel accepted or when he needs enough support to try to engage in behavior aimed at solving his problem. Finally, interpretative responses are sometimes useful in confronting another person with the impact of his behavior on you; this will be further discussed in Chapter 9. Interpretation, if carried out with skill, integrity, and empathy, can be a powerful stimulus to growth. Interpretation leads to insight, and insight is a key to better psychological living. Interpretation is one form of confrontation.

To determine your comprehension of the above material, you may wish to answer the following questions (answers on p. 139):

1. What five kinds of statements make up 80 percent of the messages sent between people?
   a. Evaluative.
   b. Problematic.
   c. Interpretative.
   d. Insensitive.
   e. Supportive.
   f. Probing.
   g. Halucinogenic.
   h. Boring.
   i. Understanding.
   j. Ingenious.

2. What response is most useful in the early stages of a relationship?
   a. Understanding.
   b. Evaluative.
   c. Unrealistic.
   d. Invaluable.

3. What response is least useful in the early stages of a relationship?
   a. Understanding.
   b. Evaluative.
   c. Reality-oriented.
   d. Snotty.

THE PHRASING OF AN ACCURATE UNDERSTANDING RESPONSE

The second important aspect of listening with understanding is the phrasing you use to paraphrase the message of the sender. The phrasing of the response may vary in the following ways:

1. *Content*. Content refers to the actual words used. Interestingly enough, responses which are essentially repetitions of the sender's statements do not communicate the receiver's understanding to the sender. It seems that just repeating a person's words gets in the way of communicating an understanding of the essential meaning of the statement. It is more effective if the receiver paraphrases the sender's message in the receiver's own words and expressions.

2. *Depth*. Depth refers to the degree that the receiver matches the depth of the sender's message in his response. You should not respond lightly to a serious statement and, correspondingly, you should not respond seriously to a shallow statement. In general, responses which match the sender's depth of feeling or which lead the sender on to a slightly greater depth of feeling are most effective.

3. *Meaning*. In the receiver's efforts to paraphrase the sender's statements he may find himself either adding meaning or omitting meaning. Some of the obvious ways in which meaning can be added are: (1) completing a sentence or thought for the sender, (2) responding to ideas which the sender has used for illustrative purposes only, and (3) interpreting the significance of a message. Perhaps the most obvious way in which meaning can be omitted is the responding only to the last thing the sender said.

4. *Language*. The receiver should keep the language he uses in his response simple in order to ensure accurate communication.

The following exercise provides you with an opportunity to classify responses according to their wording. The procedure for the exercise is as follows:

1. Each person should answer the questionnaire in the wording of an understanding response. The specific instructions are given on "Answer Sheet III," p. 253.

2. Study the categories of the understanding response given on page 136. Then categorize the responses for each item in the questionnaire as to the type of understanding response it represents. The specific instructions are given on "Answer Sheet IV," p. 255.

3. Using the scoring key on page 257, score "Answer Sheet III." Indicate the number of times you used each type of wording in the appropriate space on the answer sheet.

4. Divide into groups of three and score "Answer Sheet IV," discussing each type of wording until everyone understands it.

5. On Table 7.2 (p. 136), mark the frequency with which each member of the group used each type of wording.

6. Use the questions given on page 137 to discuss the results summarized in Table 7.2.

EXERCISE ON ACCURATE UNDERSTANDING

In this exercise (adapted from E. H. Porter, Jr., *Therapeutic Counseling* [Boston: Houghton Mifflin Company, 1950], pp. 37–40), there are nine consecutive statements made by a young person who has sought help from a friend because of his inability to keep a girl friend for any length of time. Each statement is followed by four possible responses. In considering each alternative response, read it as a tentative statement, a questioning statement which asks of the person, "Do I understand you correctly? Is this what you mean?" See the answer sheets (pp. 253 and 255) for specific instructions regarding what to do with these statements.

13. "I've come to see if you can help me get a date with Shirley. (*Pause*) I suppose if I did get a date, I'd just bungle things. Something would go wrong. At least I'd probably be without a date again next weekend."

1. You want a date, but you feel that if you do get it something would get messed up.
2. You feel that you lack self-confidence and are unable to hold onto a girl, even if you could get a date.
3. You're bothered because you can't get a girl friend, and you're turning to me for help?
4. You feel that it's pretty worthless to try again.

14. "Oh, well, I guess it's all sort of hopeless. The days go on; everybody's going out except me. (*Pause*) My dad said that when he was my age he had a date every night. (*Pause*) Maybe what's wrong with me is that I don't resemble my old man."

1. You feel that you're not quite up to it, is that it?
2. You feel that you're not dating because of your own inadequacy, is that it?

3. So you feel that this hopelessness may be something within you?

4. In other words, you just feel pretty inadequate.

15. "I wonder if you know what it feels like to sit home every night never knowing what your girl is doing. Have you ever spent the night of the Junior Prom babysitting your little sisters?"

1. It's the blows to your pride that make you feel bitter, is that it?

2. You're wondering if I can appreciate what a humiliating experience it can be.

3. You're wondering if I have ever been in such a spot.

4. It's pretty tough to miss out on so many social events.

16. "What do you think I ought to do—jump off a bridge, or look for another girl to lose?"

1. There just doesn't seem to be any way out.

2. You've just given up, is that it?

3. You're feeling discouraged now, is that it?

4. You'd like to know if I can't give you some answers?

17. "You know, last year I really thought I was going places. I was going with Gayle for four months before I had a bad break; I stood her up for—oh, well, you're probably not interested." (*Pause*)

1. You feel that to explain your bad break to me would only bore me?

2. Things looked pretty hopeful for a while, but then the bottom just dropped out, is that it?

3. You'd really like to tell me about this, but you feel uncertain about going ahead, is that it?

4. I take it you felt pretty deeply disappointed.

18. "Well, it was just that I stood her up once to go to a family dinner. I couldn't get a hold of her till the last minute to break the date, and she was pretty sore. Soon after that I was quite available again. (*Pause*) Oh, there may have been other reasons for her breaking off, but that's the one that sticks in my mind."

1. In other words, while there may have been other things involved, you feel fairly sure the most important thing was connected with your breaking that last date.

2. In other words you feel there was a direct connection between your breaking the date and being cut off.

3. You feel you were also treated unfairly, and you just can't get it out of your head.

4. That's the reason that sticks in your mind, but you feel there may have been other reasons.

19. "Well, maybe it's just that I'm no good. I get good girls—but after a while I get that old fear of losing them."

1. You feel this fear of losing your girl plays a part in making you lose the girl, is that it?

2. As I get it, this fear of losing out makes you wonder if it's not that you just don't have what it takes to make it.

3. You get good girls but you worry about losing them, is that it?

4. I'm just wondering if there isn't something that might be wrong.

20. (*Angrily*) "Did you ever have anything grab onto you so you couldn't shake it loose? Well, mister, I have! I've got a habit that if I don't cut it out, I'm going to ruin myself and my home—and everything."

1. This thing will just drive you out of your head unless you can shake it.

2. It's a habit you can't shake and will be harmful.

3. This thing really bugs you.

4. You feel you just don't have enough guts to meet this thing.

21. "You see, it all started last year. We had a club—all fellas—and we used to go out and drink beer. We did that every week—even during the summer. (*Pause*) Well, beer got to be quite a habit with me. My folks were German and we always had it around the house, so they didn't care. Well, that was okay, but when I started dating and found out I couldn't hold my girl, then I began to drink more and more. Even my buddies thought I was going to the dogs and told me to lay off. (*Pause*) If you could just get me to quit drinking, I'd be okay."

1. You began to lose girls and then started drinking too much?

2. This drinking is something you want to get over.

3. You feel that you used drink to drown your disappointment in your-self?

4. It may have started out innocently enough, but now it's become something that is a real problem to you.

TYPES OF PHRASING OF AN UNDERSTANDING RESPONSE

Now that you have completed "Answer Sheet III," study and discuss the following categories of the understanding response. Do not proceed until you are sure you understand each of the categories.

In the beginning of this section we discussed four aspects of an understanding response: content, depth, meaning, and language. The above questionnaire focuses upon two of these dimensions—content (either identical or paraphrased) and meaning (either partial or additional). In the above questionnaire all of the alternatives following the statements are so phrased as to appear to be attempts to communicate an understanding intent. For each statement, however, the alternatives differ in the following ways:

Identical Content (I): a response in which the attempt at understanding is implemented in large part by simply repeating the same words used by the sender.

Paraphrasing Content (P): a response in which the attempt at understanding is implemented by rephrasing in fresh words the gist of the sender's expression without changing either the meaning or the feeling tone.

Shallow or Partial Meaning (S): a response in which the attempt at understanding is implemented in a limited way by involving only a part of what the sender expressed or by "undercutting" or "watering down" the feeling tone expressed.

Additional Meaning (A): a response in which the attempt at understanding actually goes beyond the meaning of the sender and adds meaning not expressed by the sender.

TABLE 7.2 THE FREQUENCY WITH WHICH THE GROUP MEMBERS USED EACH TYPE OF RESPONSE

Frequency of Response	Type of Responses			
	I	P	S	A
0–1	_____	_____	_____	_____
2–3	_____	_____	_____	_____
4–5	_____	_____	_____	_____
6–7	_____	_____	_____	_____
8–9	_____	_____	_____	_____

After you have finished the procedure for scoring both answer sheets, mark the frequency with which each member of the group used each type of phrasing. In the group, discuss the results summarized in Table 7.2 and the consequences of using each type of phrasing. The following questions may be helpful:

1. What type of phrasing was most commonly used by the members of the group?
2. What would be your feelings if a person used each type of phrasing in discussing your problems and concerns?
3. How may I develop my skills in paraphrasing to ensure the most effective phrasing of my response?

PRACTICING THE PHRASING OF AN UNDERSTANDING RESPONSE

The following exercise provides you with practice in the phrasing of an understanding response. The exercise consists of two parts, one in which you are given a problem statement and you write down what you would say, and another in which you and another person make statements and practice with each other giving an appropriately phrased understanding response. The procedure for the exercise is as follows:

1. Read the following paragraphs and write an understanding response for each one. Do this by yourself. Be sure your response matches the paragraph in content, depth, language and meaning.

   a. "I'm really upset! That stupid professor gave me a *C* on my research paper! I worked on it for six weeks and it was twice as long as the paper Joe turned in, yet he got an *A*. That paper presented a lot of learning on my part. And he had the nerve to give me a *C*! What does he want anyway? Or is it that I'm just dumb?"

   Response: _____

   _____

   _____

   _____

   b. "I need your help. There's a new girl who just moved in next door to you that I think I know. She may be a girl I dated several years ago; but I'm not sure since I haven't been able to get a close look at her. If she is the same girl I want to meet her; if she isn't the same girl, I don't want to meet her. Can you find out her name, telephone, and where she grew up?"

Response: _____

_____

_____

_____

2. Divide into pairs. Discuss each other's responses and make suggestions as to how they might be improved.

3. Think of a problem you are having with a friend or a member of your family. It may be a major problem or a minor problem. Each person in the pair should share his problem; the receiver gives an understanding response which is appropriate in content, depth, language, and meaning.

4. In the pairs, give each other feedback concerning the appropriateness of the content, depth, language, and meaning of the understanding responses. You may wish to continue practicing the phrasing of the understanding response until you have mastered it to your satisfaction. This can be done by consciously applying it in your everyday conversations or by pairing up with a member of your group and setting specific practice times for the two of you to increase your skills.

CHECKLIST OF SKILLS

1. I have mastered the use of the following types of responses:

_____ Evaluative.

_____ Interpretive.

_____ Supportive.

_____ Probing.

_____ Understanding.

2. I need more work on the following types of responses in order to effectively master their use:

_____ Evaluative.

_____ Interpretative.

_____ Supportive.

_____ Probing.

_____ Understanding.

3. I have mastered the phrasing of the understanding response on the following dimensions:

_____ Content (paraphrasing rather than repeating).

_____ Meaning (neither adding to nor subtracting from the original meaning).

_____ Depth.

_____ Language.

4. I need more work in phrasing understanding responses on the following dimensions:

_____ Content.

_____ Meaning.

_____ Depth.

_____ Language.

ANSWERS

Page 118: 1: *b;* 2: *a, c*
Page 131: 1: *a, c, e, f, i;* 2: *a;* 3: *b*

Acceptance of Self and Others

8

In this chapter we focus upon accepting yourself and communicating acceptance to other people. The objectives of this chapter are to increase your self-acceptance and to increase your skills in expressing acceptance to others.

THE FOUR POSITIONS IN ACCEPTANCE OF SELF AND OTHERS

Harris (1967) states that there are four possible positions held with respect to yourself and others. They are:

1. *I'm Not O.K., You're O.K.* In this position the person feels at the mercy of other people. He feels a great need for support, acceptance, and recognition. The person in this position hopes that others who are O.K. will give him support and acceptance, and he worries about what he has to do to get others to give him the support and acceptance he needs. He communicates to others that he is self-rejecting and needs their acceptance and support.

2. *I'm Not O.K., You're Not O.K.* In this position there is no source of support and acceptance, not from oneself or from others. Individuals in this position give up all hope of being happy and may withdraw from all relationships. Even if others try to give support and acceptance, the person in this position rejects it because they "are not O.K." He communicates to others both self-rejection and rejection of them.

3. *I'm O.K., You're Not O.K.* The person in this position rejects all support and acceptance from others, but provides it for himself. He feels that he will be all right if others leave him alone. He is ultra-independent and doesn't want to get involved with others. He also rejects the support and acceptance of others because they "are not O.K." He communicates to others that he is fine, but they are not.

4. *I'm O.K., You're O.K.* In this position the person decides that he is worthwhile and valuable and that other people are also worthwhile and valuable. He accepts himself and responds to acceptance from others. He can give acceptance and receive acceptance. He is free to get involved in meaningful relationships. He communicates to others that he appreciates his own strengths and appreciates their strengths. This is the position that everyone should strive to be in. This is the position which facilitates the development of close, meaningful relationships with others.

Every time you relate to another person you are communicating one of the above positions. Most people relate to everyone from the same position; that is, how they feel about themselves and others does not change greatly from relationship to relationship, and it governs everything they do. It is important for you to make the conscious decision that you are going to relate to others from the fourth position and strive to do that. Only when you accept yourself and accept other people can you build and maintain mature meaningful relationships.

In this chapter we will first focus upon the achievement of the feeling and conviction "I'm O.K." We will then focus upon the skills involved in communicating "You're O.K." to other people.

SELF-ACCEPTANCE

Self-acceptance is a high regard for yourself, or, conversely, a lack of cynicism about yourself. Generally, a high level of self-acceptance is reflected in a high level of quality of personal adjustment (see Hamachek, 1971). A person's mental health depends deeply on the quality of his feelings about himself. Just as an individual must maintain a healthy view of the world around him, so must he learn to perceive himself in positive ways. Psychologically healthy individuals see themselves as liked, wanted, acceptable to others, capable, and worthy. Highly self-critical individuals are more anxious, more insecure, and possibly more cynical and depressed than self-accepting individuals. The self-accepting person views the world as a more congenial place than the self-rejecting person and is less defensive towards others and about himself because of it. Carl Rogers (1951) considers self-acceptance to be crucial for psychological health and growth. It is not the individuals who feel that they are liked, wanted, acceptable to others, capable, and worthy who are found in prisons and mental hospitals; it is those who feel deeply inadequate, un-liked, unwanted, unacceptable, and unable.

In order for you to grow and develop psychologically, therefore, you must be self-accepting. To help others grow and develop psychologically, you must help others become more self-accepting. To develop your potential for happiness and good relationships you must achieve and maintain a high level of self-acceptance. A self-rejecting person is usually unhappy and unable to form and maintain good relationships.

There is considerable evidence that self-acceptance and the acceptance of others are related (see Hamachek, 1971). Individuals who are self-accepting are usually more accepting of others. This means that if you think well of yourself you are likely to think well of others, and that if you disapprove of yourself you are likely to disapprove of others. In addition, things you try to hide from yourself about yourself you often are very critical of in others. A person who supresses hostility may be highly critical of people who express hostility. A person who suppresses sexual feelings may be highly critical of individuals who are more open with their sexual feelings. If you recognize and accept your feelings, you are usually more accepting of such emotional expressions in others. The self-accepting person views the world as a more congenial place than the self-rejecting person and is less defensive towards others and about himself because of it. We will, then, be focusing upon how we may increase our self-acceptance and, therefore, become more accepting of others.

Your self-acceptance is built by knowing that others are accepting of you. The acceptance of you by others plays a critical role in increasing your self-acceptance, especially the acceptance of you by those you care about and respect. One of the ways in which you may become more self-accepting is to feel that other people whom you like and respect accept you. We will be focusing upon how to express acceptance towards others in order to help them increase their self-acceptance.

Your self-acceptance can set up self-fulfilling prophecies where your expectations concerning how other people are going to view you are actually confirmed as a result of your behavior. For example, a self-rejecting person expects to be rejected by others and will tend to reject others; as a result of his rejection, the people with whom he is interacting will reciprocate by rejecting him; the person's original expectations are then confirmed. A self-accepting person, on the other hand, will expect to be accepted by others and will tend to accept other people; they, in turn, will tend to reciprocate by being accepting of him; his original expectations are then confirmed. It is through such self-fulfilling prophecies that one may build good relationships or may experience real difficulty in making a friend.

To increase your self-acceptance, you must self-disclose in order to let other people know you and to experience acceptance by others. People are not accepting of individuals they do not know—most often they are neutral or indifferent. The relationship among self-acceptance, self-disclosure, and being accepted by other people is important. If you do not self-disclose, you cannot be accepted by others and your self-acceptance will not be increased. Paradoxically, not only is your self-acceptance increased by self-disclosing (and subsequently being accepted by others) but how easy it is for you to self-disclose is related to your level of self-acceptance. The greater your self-acceptance, the easier it will be for you to self-disclose. Self-confidence about your worth reduces the risks involved in self-disclosing. Self-acceptance is the key to reducing anxiety and fears about vulnerability resulting from self-disclosure. If you are afraid to let others know you, or anxious about the reactions others may have to your self-disclosure, you will not be open and disclosing, and, therefore, you will not be able to facilitate the development of good relationships with other people. If you are self-rejecting, you will find self-disclosure very risky

The deepest conviction a self-rejecting person has is that once he is known he will be rejected and unloved. Before a self-rejecting person can have this conviction dissolved and experience more acceptance from himself and other persons, he must take the risk of disclosing himself. It is important for your self-acceptance that you are honest, genuine, and authentic in your self-disclosing. If you hide information about yourself or selectively try to create an impression on other people, the acceptance they give you may actually decrease your self-acceptance; you will know that it is your "mask" other people like and accept, not your "real" self. Being accepted for a "lie" leads only to self-rejection. It is only as you discover that you are loved for what you are, not for what you pretend to be or for the masks you hide behind, that you can begin to feel you are actually a person worthy of respect and love.

CHARACTERISTICS OF SELF-ACCEPTING INDIVIDUALS

A person who has a strong, self-accepting attitude presents the following behavioral picture (Hamachek, 1971):

1. He believes strongly in certain values and principles and is willing to defend them even in the face of strong group opinion. He feels personally secure enough, however, to modify them if new experience and evidence suggest he is in error.
2. He is capable of acting on his own best judgment without feeling excessively guilty or regretting his actions if others disapprove of what he has done.

3. He does not spend undue time worrying about what is coming tomorrow, what has happened in the past, or what is taking place in the present.

4. He has confidence in his ability to deal with problems, even in the face of failure and setbacks.

5. He feels equal to others as a person, not superior or inferior, irrespective of the differences in specific abilities, family backgrounds, or attitudes of others toward him.

6. He is able to take for granted that he is a person of interest and value to others, at least to those with whom he chooses to associate.

7. He can accept praise without the pretense of false modesty and compliments without feeling guilty.

8. He is inclined to resist the efforts of others to dominate him.

9. He is able to accept the idea and admit to others that he is capable of feeling a wide range of impulses and desires, ranging from being angry to being loving, from being sad to being happy, from feeling deep resentment to feeling deep acceptance.

10. He is able to genuinely enjoy himself in a wide variety of activities involving work, play, creative self-expression, companionship, or loafing.

11. He is sensitive to the needs of others, to accepted social customs, and particularly to the idea that he cannot enjoy himself at the expense of others.

STRENGTH-BUILDING EXERCISE

One way to build self-acceptance is to increase our awareness of our strengths. We all have many different strengths upon which we base our interactions with other people. All individuals have solid strengths which are presently unidentified and unused. Through identification of these strengths we may increase our ability to relate to other people. The word *strength* refers to any skill, talent, ability, or personal trait which helps you to function more productively. Through identifying your present strengths you may increase your regard for yourself and, therefore, increase your self-acceptance. In addition, you may explore and develop your potential strengths into solid strengths, you may intensify your presently known strengths by practicing them, and you may restructure weaknesses into strengths.

In this exercise you will concentrate upon identifying your strengths and how they can be used most productively to build close, personal relationships. The objectives of the exercise are to increase your self-acceptance through the increased awareness of your strengths and to increase your awareness of how your strengths may be used to develop fulfilling relationships with other individuals. In this exercise you will be asked to discuss your strengths openly with the other group members. This is no place for modesty; an inferiority complex or the unwillingness to be open about your positive attributes is not a strength. You are not being asked to brag, only to be realistic and open about the strengths which you possess. The procedure for the exercise is as follows:

1. Think of all the things that you do well, all the things which you are proud of having done, all the things for which you feel a sense of accomplishment. List all your positive accomplishments, your successes, of the past. Be specific.

   My positive accomplishments are: _____

   _____

   _____

   _____

   _____

   _____

   _____

   _____

   _____

   _____

   _____

   _____

   _____

   _____

   _____

   _____

   _____

2. Divide into pairs and share your past accomplishments with each

other. Then, with the help of your partner, examine your past successes to identify the strengths you utilized to achieve them.

My personal strengths are: _____

_____

_____

_____

_____

_____

_____

_____

_____

_____

_____

_____

_____

_____

_____

3. In the group as a whole, each person should share the full list of his strengths. Then ask the group, "What additional strengths do you see in my life?" The group then adds to your list other qualities, skills, characteristics that you have overlooked or undervalued. The feedback should be specific; that is, if one member tells another he has a strength, he must back his feedback up with some evidence of behavior which demonstrates the strength.

4. After every group member has shared his strengths and received feedback on what further strengths others see in his life, each member should then ask the group, "What might be keeping me from utilizing all my strengths?" The group then explores the ways in which you can free yourself from factors which limit the utilization of your strengths.

The barriers to my utilizing my strengths are: _____

_____

_____

_____

_____

_____

5. Think about your past successes and your strengths. Think about how your strengths may be utilized to improve the number or quality of your close relationships. Then set a goal for the next week concerning how you may improve either the number or the quality of your close relationships. Plan how the utilization of your strengths will help you accomplish this goal.

My goal is: _____

_____

_____

_____

My strengths involved are: _____

_____

_____

_____

The ways in which I will utilize my strengths to accomplish my goal are: _____

_____

_____

_____

I will know that my goal is accomplished when: _____

_____

_____

_____

EXERCISE IN GAINING ACCEPTANCE

Sometimes other persons do not just give you acceptance, you have to earn it. We often spend a great deal of time and energy trying to gain the acceptance of individuals we like and admire. This exercise provides an opportunity to experience gaining acceptance from the group nonverbally. The procedure for the exercise is as follows:

1. One member volunteers to be an outsider. The other members of the group form a tight circle by locking arms and pressing close to each other's sides.

2. The outsider has to break into the group by forcing his way to the center of the circle. This is a quite active exercise. You should, therefore, be careful not to hurt anyone by becoming too rough. Anyone with a physical injury should not take part in this exercise.

3. After everyone who wishes to has been an outsider discuss the experience. The discussion may center upon:
   a. How did you react to being an outsider? What did you learn about yourself from the experience?
   b. How did you react to trying to keep the outsiders from gaining entry into the group? What did you learn about yourself from the experience?

EXERCISE IN EXPRESSING ACCEPTANCE NONVERBALLY

The purpose of this exercise is for each person in the group to have an opportunity to experience fully the acceptance felt for him by other members. At the same time, the members of the group are given an opportunity to express acceptance nonverbally. The procedure for the exercise is as follows:

1. One member volunteers to stand in the center of a circle made up by the other members of the group. He is to shut his eyes and stand silently.

2. The other members of the group are all to approach him and express their positive feelings nonverbally in whatever way they wish. This

may take the form of hugging, stroking, massaging, lifting, or whatever each person feels.

3. After everyone who wishes to has been in the center of the circle, the group may wish to discuss the experience. The discussion may center on the following two areas:

   a. How did it feel to receive so much acceptance and affection? What were the reactions of each person in the center. Was it a tense situation for you or was it an enjoyable one? Why do you react as you do? What did you learn about yourself?

   b. How did it feel to give so much acceptance and affection to other members of the group? What are your reactions to such giving? Why do you react this way? What did you learn about yourself from this experience?

ACCEPTANCE OF OTHER INDIVIDUALS

The communication of mutual acceptance is vital to developing and maintaining close, personal relationships. The mutual communication of acceptance leads to feelings of *psychological safety;* that is, to feelings that no matter what you do or what you disclose about yourself, the other person in the relationship will react in an accepting and nonevaluative way. In order to build close, satisfying relationships, therefore, you must be able to communicate acceptance to other individuals. They must feel that you are communicating to them, "You're O.K." There are times when the communication of such acceptance will lead to a generalized feeling in the other person of being supported. There are other times when the individual has taken a risk in disclosing something of importance, and your ability to communicate acceptance is crucial for the development of trust and for further self-disclosure in the relationship. Although it may now seem like communicating acceptance is a hard thing to do, with an understanding of what skills are involved and with a little practice you will be able to communicate acceptance quite comfortably.

There are two major skills involved in communicating acceptance to another individual. The first is *listening with understanding* to the other individual. When you listen with understanding to the self-disclosures or ideas of another person, you come to understand the issue from his point of view. Unless you understand what the other person is saying, you can not respond in an accepting way. You cannot accept what you do not know or understand. Thus, listening with understanding ensures that you will know what the other person is trying to communicate in order to respond in an accepting way. In addition, listening with understanding communicates to the other person that you sincerely want to understand him. This desire to understand the other person is, under most conditions, perceived to be a sign of caring about the other person and a willingness to take his ideas and feelings seriously. The other person, therefore, becomes less defensive in his communications to you and more willing to take risks in self-disclosure which builds mutual trust in the relationship.

The second skill involved in communicating acceptance to another person is the *expression of warmth and liking*. There is almost universal recognition that a degree of warmth in interpersonal relationships is absolutely essential for psychological growth. The expression of warmth and liking is vital to building a climate of psychological safety in the relationship and a feeling on the part of the other person that you accept him as a person. Without the communication of positive regard you cannot communicate acceptance to another person.

There are two types of acceptance you may communicate to the other person: antecedent acceptance and consequent acceptance. Encouragement for the other person to take risks in self-disclosure or to build a closer relationship is *antecedent acceptance* while expressing acceptance to the other person following his risk-taking in self-disclosure or building a closer relationship is *consequent acceptance*.

The primary means of expressing antecedent acceptance is to communicate unconditional warmth or liking for the person. *Unconditional warmth* is communicating to the other person that you have a deep and genuine regard for him as a person which allows him complete freedom in expressing the ways in which he is different from other individuals, in other words, allows him to be who and what he is. This unconditional warmth does not mean that you will approve of everything the other person does. Approval is quite different from accepting someone as a person you care for. We usually do not want our friends to overlook, discount, or approve of all our behavior no matter what we do. A sign of true friendship is often the other person's willingness to tell us when he disapproves of our behavior while still communicating that he accepts us as a person. We all behave in ways which we disapprove of later, and we would not want our friends to approve such behavior either. Disapproving of our behavior, however, does not mean rejecting us as persons.

Another means of ensuring antecedent acceptance is by building a high level of trust in the relationship. As was discussed in Chapter 3, mutual trust is absolutely essential for a friendship to grow and develop. Ensuring that the other person trusts you to respond with acceptance and support to his risk-taking in self-disclosure, and despite the fact that you may not approve of all of his behavior, is another primary means of expressing antecedent acceptance.

If the communication of antecedent acceptance is crucial for encouraging individuals to take the risks necessary to build a closer, more fulfilling relationship, then the communication of consequent acceptance keeps the relationship building and growing. Consequent acceptance reinforces the other person's behavior and increases the frequency with which the other person engages in behaviors that increase the quality of the relationship.

Consequent acceptance is a reinforcement for positive behavior, such as self-disclosure and the expression of feeling, and as such, it will be discussed at greater length in the chapter on the use of reinforcement. For the present, it should be noted that the more immediately the communication of acceptance follows the other person's risk-taking behavior, the more impact it will have upon encouraging him to engage in positive risk-taking behavior in the future. The response of listening with understanding and the expression of warmth and liking both are ways of giving immediate reinforcement to the other person's behavior.

In addition to the skills of listening with understanding and expressing warmth and liking, the unspoken or tacit ways in which your behavior indicates acceptance of the other person are important in expressing antecedent and consequent acceptance. Being available when the other person needs help, going out of your way to give him support or help, asking him to help you when you need it, spending time with the other person are all ways in which your behavior *tacitly communicates acceptance*. Such tacit communication is an important aspect of building close, satisfying relationships.

FAILURES IN ACCEPTANCE

There are three ways in which you may fail to indicate any real acceptance for another person. The first is to give cliché or ritualistic acceptance. Our language is filled with socially appropriate clichés expressive of acceptance such as these: "I know how you feel." "Is there anything I can do?" "You must feel awful." "You're so strong and wonderful." The difference between a statement that expresses genuine acceptance and a cliché is the amount of feeling and sincerity expressed in the statement and whether the statement opens up a discussion of the other person's feelings or closes off such a discussion.

The second is whether the acceptance is expressed to the other because of the quality of your relationship or whether you would do the same thing for anyone. Cheap acceptance which you hand out to anyone and everyone does not communicate any real acceptance of the other person. Cheap acceptance is similar to being a Red Cross worker who rushes to give aid to everyone she sees. Meaningful acceptance is based upon your relationship with the other person and should reflect either the present quality of the relationship or the desire to build a closer relationship.

Finally, the greatest failure to communicate acceptance is silence. When you interact with another person, silence is often taken as a sign of indifference and unwillingness to commit yourself to the relationship. Certainly, silence does not communicate either antecedent or consequent acceptance to the other person, and it may communicate consequent rejection.

COMMUNICATING ACCEPTANCE TO OTHER INDIVIDUALS

The purpose of this exercise is to provide you with an opportunity to practice communicating acceptance to another person. The skills involved in expressing acceptance are listening with understanding and the expression of warmth. In this exercise you will conduct a discussion in which you practice listening with understanding and the expression of warmth. The procedure is as follows:

1. Divide into trios. Two individuals will be engaged in a discussion; one person will observe. The role of the discussants is to express acceptance to each other. The role of the observer is to give the two discussants feedback concerning how successfully they communicated acceptance to each other. An observation sheet is provided for the observer's use on p. 259.

2. The two discussants spend 10 minutes discussing how their current close friendships were initiated and developed. Or they may discuss any topic that is of real interest to the two of them; do not spend more than one minute, however, on the selection of a topic to discuss. During the discussion the two participants should be practicing both listening with understanding and expressing warmth. To listen with understanding is to paraphrase the other person's expressed feelings and ideas in your own words without any indication of approval or disapproval; this involves listening for meaning as well as listening to the other's words. To express warmth is to describe your feelings and to use the nonverbal cues of facial expression, tone of voice, posture, and so on in your discussion with your partner.

3. At the end of the 10-minute discussion, the observer and the two discussants give the two discussants feedback concerning how well they expressed acceptance to each other. Be specific.

4. The trio next switches roles so that one of the previous discussants is now the observer and the other two members conduct a discussion.

Follow the instructions given in Step 2. This time discuss what your greatest fears and hopes concerning initiating friendships are.

5. Conduct a feedback session according to the instructions given in Step 3.

6. Switch roles once more and conduct a discussion on why you need friends. Follow the instructions given in Steps 2 and 3.

LEVEL OF ACCEPTANCE IN YOUR GROUP

What is the level of acceptance in your group? You may wish to get everyone's opinion by completing the following questionnaire and summarizing the results. The purpose of this exercise is to provide a way in which the level of acceptance in your group may be assessed and discussed. The procedure is as follows:

1. Each member of the group fill out the following questionnaire.

2. The results are tabulated in the "Summary Table," p. 156.

3. Discuss the conclusions that can be drawn from the results.

4. What is contributing to the present high or low level of acceptance in the group?

5. How may the level of acceptance in the group be increased?

GROUP CLIMATE QUESTIONNAIRE

Think about the ways in which the fellow-members of your group normally behave towards you. In the parentheses in front of the items below place the number corresponding to your perceptions of the group as a whole, using the following scale:

5 = They *always* can be counted upon to behave this way.

4 = They *typically* behave this way.

3 = They *usually* behave this way.

2 = They *seldom* behave this way.

1 = They *rarely* behave this way.

0 = They *never* behave this way.

I would expect my fellow group members to:

1. (____)————————————level with me.

2. ————(____)————————get the drift of what I am trying to say.

3.* ————————(____)————interrupt or ignore my comments.

4. ——————————(____)———accept me for what I am.

5. (____)——————————————feel free to let me know when I bug them.

6.* ————(____)————————misconstrue things I say or do.

7. ————————(____)————be interested in me.

8. ——————————(____)———provide an atmosphere where I can be myself.

9.* (____)————————————keep things to themselves to spare my feelings.

10. ————(____)————————perceive what kind of person I really am.

11. ————————(____)————include me in what's going on.

12.* ——————————(____)———act judgmental with me.

13. (____)——————————————be completely frank with me.

14. ————(____)————————recognize readily when something is bothering me.

15. ————————(____)————respect me as a person, apart from my skills or status.

16.* ——————————(____)———ridicule me or disapprove if I show my peculiarities.

———————————————

(____) Genuineness with me.

(____) Understanding of me.

(____) Valuing of me.

(____) Accepting of me.

Add the total number of points in each column. Items with starred (*) numbers are reversed in the scoring; subtract the rating given to each from 5 before entering these scores in the following table.

Collect the results of the questionnaire on unsigned sheets of paper so that no one's responses can be identified. Then summarize the results in the "Summary Table" and discuss the questions given on page 154.

SUMMARY TABLE

Score	Genuineness	Understanding	Valuing	Accepting
0–4	_____	_____	_____	_____
5–8	_____	_____	_____	_____
9–12	_____	_____	_____	_____
13–16	_____	_____	_____	_____
17–20	_____	_____	_____	_____

MATCHING

How well do you remember the material discussed in this chapter? You may wish to match the elements of the two columns below to review the content presented on self-acceptance and acceptance of others (answers on p. 157):

_____ 1. Self-acceptance.

a. Any skill, talent, ability, or personal trait that helps you to function more productively.

_____ 2. Self-fulfilling prophecy.

b. Clichés, Red-Crossing, and silence.

_____ 3. Psychological safety.

c. Encouraging self-disclosure from another person.

_____ 4. Antecedent acceptance.

d. A high regard for yourself.

_____ 5. Unconditional warmth.

e. A deep and genuine regard for another person which allows him to be who he is.

_____ 6. Failure to accept other person.

f. Expressing acceptance to another person following his risking self-disclosure.

_____ 7. Consequent acceptance.

g. An expectation that comes true because it influenced the situation.

_____ 8. Expressing acceptance to another person.

h. Attempting to view the ideas and feelings of another person from his point of view.

_____ 9. Personal strength.

i. Feeling that other people will react to you in accepting and nonevaluative ways.

_____10. Listening with understanding.

j. Listening with understanding and expressing warmth and liking.

CHECKLIST OF SKILLS

1. I have mastered the following:

    _____ Awareness of my strengths.

    _____ Recognizing and expressing my feelings.

    _____ Expressing acceptance to other individuals.

    _____ Awareness of other people's acceptance of me.

    _____ Communicating "I'm O.K., you're O.K."

2. I need more work on the following:

    _____ Awareness of my strengths.

    _____ Recognizing and expressing my feelings.

    _____ Expressing acceptance to other individuals.

    _____ Awareness of other people's acceptance of me.

    _____ Communicating "I'm O.K., you're O.K."

ANSWERS

Pages 156–157:   *1: d; 2: g; 3: i; 4: c; 5: e; 6: b; 7: f; 8: j; 9: a; 10: h*

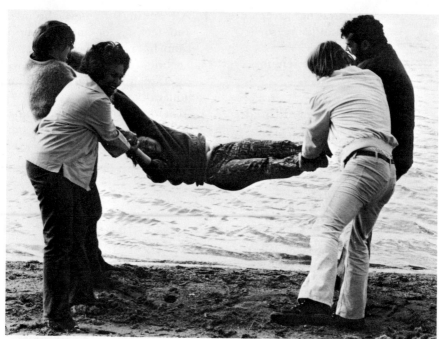

Constructive Confrontation

In building and maintaining a close relationship it is of utmost importance that you be honest with the other person. Friendships are built by building trust, expressing warmth, support, and acceptance, but inevitably there are times when you become angry with the other person or feel that he is behaving in a way that is destructive to himself, to you, or to other people. At this point we need to reflect upon the meaning of friendship and the meaning of being committed to another person. Which is the true friend: a person who ignores the destructive behavior of another person, or one who risks rejection by confronting the other person with the consequences of his behavior in order to help him not make the same mistake over and over again? If you are a person's friend, do you ignore his interpersonal mistakes or do you confront him with his mistakes in a way which facilitates his learning not to make the same mistake in the future? In this chapter we examine the skills involved in constructively confronting other individuals with the consequences of their behavior.

INTERPERSONAL CONFRONTATION

Constructive confrontations in a relationship are of high potential value, both in improving our interpersonal effectiveness and in improving the quality of the relationship. Productive change often results from challenges to become more effective in interpersonal situations. Individuals concerned with their interpersonal skills learn to challenge themselves in order to continually improve their effectiveness; they welcome, therefore, being confronted by their friends as a challenge for productive behavioral changes. When confrontations are skillful and responsible, they are a powerful force for increased interpersonal effectiveness and growth.

A *confrontation* may be defined as a deliberate attempt to help another person examine the consequences of some aspect of his behavior. It is an invitation to self-examination. A confrontation originates from a desire on the part of the confronter to involve himself more deeply with the person he is confronting. Confrontation is a way of expressing concern for another person and a wish to increase the mutual involvement in the relationship. The first rule of confrontation is, "Do not confront another person if you do not intend to increase your involvement with him."

The purpose of a confrontation is to free the person being confronted to engage in more fruitful or less destructive behavior. In most cases this means that you should confront a person in such a way that the person being confronted takes the feedback seriously but does not become so defensive that he refuses to accept or use the feedback.

The decision to confront another person is made upon two major aspects of the relationship:

1. The quality of the relationship; generally, the stronger the relationship the more powerful the confrontation may be.
2. The perceived ability of the person being confronted to act upon the confrontation; if at the moment a person's anxiety level is high or his motivation or ability to change is low, the confrontation will not be utilized as an invitation for self-examination, and therefore it should not take place.

The strength of the wording of a confrontation can be important in affecting its impact upon the person being confronted. In its simplest form, a confrontation is a suggestion or request that the person being confronted change his behavior in some way. It is usually a mistake for the confronter to demand that the other change his behavior. Even if the confronter does not intend to play God or omnipotent father, he may give the impression that he is doing so, which tends to undermine any value that the confrontation may otherwise have.

Since no one can predict with absolute certainty whether a change in another's behavior will benefit him, there is always an element of hypothesis in every confrontation. How certain you feel should dictate the strength of the wording of your confrontation. If another person, for example, is engaging in quite self-destructive behavior or behavior quite destructive of others, you may request or strongly suggest that he change his behavior; for milder behaviors, however, the confrontation may be quite tentative or softly worded.

As we said in Chapter 2, the effectiveness of our behavior depends in large measure on the feedback we receive from other people. Getting feedback from other persons not only provides an opportunity to increase your self-awareness, but it also helps you determine the consequences of your behavior. The ability to receive feedback is part of the functioning of any healthy, effective individual. It is the capacity for receiving feedback which enables you continually to adjust your behavior and reactions so as to achieve the maximum possible fulfillment in your relationships with other people. It is through confronting other people with the consequences of their behavior that you help them to grow and develop; it is through other people confronting you that you increase your interpersonal effectiveness. If you cannot obtain information on the consequences of your behavior, you cannot modify your behavior to make it more effective.

You may wish to test your understanding of the above material by answering the following questions (answers on p. 169):

1. The first rule of confrontation is:
   a. Do not confront another person if you do not intend to get involved with him.
   b. Do not confront another person if he is not ready for it.
   c. Do not confront another person for past behavior.
   d. Do not confront another person unless he is confronting you.

2. The purpose of confrontation is:
   a. To indulge in a freeing of your inner feelings.
   b. To free the person being confronted to engage in better behavior.
   c. To free you to engage in confrontative behavior.
   d. To show the other person how nasty you can be.

3. What two aspects of the relationship is the decision to confront made upon?
   a. The trust level.
   b. The nature of the behavior to which the confrontation is directed.
   c. The quality of your confrontation skills.
   d. The ability of the person being confronted to act upon the confrontation.
   e. The quality of the relationship.

4. What determines how strongly you word a confrontation?
   a. How certain you feel.

b. How closed the other person is.

c. How much you want to risk in the relationship.

TYPES OF CONFRONTATIONS

There are basically two types of confrontations, informational and interpretative. The most basic form of confrontation is to communicate to another person some information concerning your perception of his behavior and its consequences and your reaction to his behavior. Ideally, this type of confrontation is the communication of correct and meaningful information by a concerned observer to a willing receiver in order that the receiver may engage in and grow through self-examination and subsequent behavioral change. An informational confrontation is in many cases the same as providing constructive feedback, and the rules for feedback presented in Chapter 2 should be followed. It is informational confrontations that promote increases in interpersonal effectiveness.

In addition to providing information, interpretations of the other person's behavior can be powerful stimuli to growth if they are communicated with skill, integrity, and empathy. Interpretation potentially leads to insight on the part of the person being confronted, and insight into oneself is supposedly a key to better psychological health. Interpretations are valuable to the extent that they are points of departure for action leading to growth by the person being confronted. The value of the interpretation is measured by the extent to which it helps the person being confronted examine his behavior and modify it in ways that improve his ability to involve himself with other people. The characteristics of an interpretative confrontation are:

1. Empathy—the confronter must understand the issues that are central to the other person's behavior and life style.

2. Timing—the confrontation must be timed so that the person being confronted is open to receiving the interpretation without becoming overly defensive.

3. Relatedness—the confrontation must be related to the situation in which the two people are engaged; it should not appear unexpectedly.

4. Concise—the confrontation should be concisely stated and to the point; long and ambiguous statements have an air of finality and tend to lose the receiver.

5. Authenticity—the confronter must be able to communicate a genuine and sincere interest in the well-being of the person being confronted.

6. Tentativeness—an interpretation is a hypothesis about the other person's behavior, not a self-evident fact.

When engaging in an interpretative confrontation, it is important to remember that an interpretation is a hypothesis about the other person's behavior. It is an inference based upon fact (the observed behavior of the person being confronted which can be verified by other observers), the feelings of the confronter arising from the impact of the other person's behavior on him, and the concepts and theories the confronter uses to analyze behavior. Thus you should not present an interpretation of the other person's behavior as self-evident fact, but rather as an inference, which may or may not be correct. You can, however, present the degree of your sureness that your interpretation is correct. The important point to remember is that in a relationship facts should be presented as facts, feelings as feelings, and inferences as inferences. You should avoid confusing feelings and inferences as facts.

In the use of informational and interpretative confrontations, you may confront a person with his strengths and constructive resources or with his weaknesses and shortcomings. A general rule to follow is that in helping a person to change constructively, you build upon his strengths and resources. Focusing upon a person's weaknesses and deficiencies can lead to discouragement, negative self-attitudes, and feelings of being self-defeating rather than to confidence in one's ability to grow and develop. Even when a person is engaging in behavior that is having disastrous consequences, it is possible to confront a person with underutilizing his strengths.

You may also want to confront a person when there is a discrepancy between what the person feels about his behavior and himself and how you perceive his behavior and its consequences. Many times people misperceive the impact of their behavior upon other individuals or underestimate their worth and abilities. When you see this happening you may wish to confront the other person.

CONSTRUCTIVE EXPRESSION OF ANGER

There are times in a relationship that you have to express anger in order to be honest about your reactions to another person's behavior. There are times when you may be able to confront another person more effectively if you express anger than if you express invariant warmth. Many times relationships are strengthened by the experiencing of an open confrontation involving anger that ends in increased closeness and affection. In building and maintaining a close friendship with another person, it is important that emotions such as anger can be expressed in ways which eventually increase the quality of the relationship. It is only through the solution of relationship problems that two individuals increase their trust in each other's abilities to cope with future strains in the relationship. It is for this reason that one noted psychiatrist, in discussing good marriages stated, "A fight a day keeps the marriage counselor away."

When is it constructive to express anger about another person's behavior? The implications of a study by Johnson (1971b) are that if you feel anger about another person's behavior, the authentic expression of that anger followed by the reaffirmation of the warmth you feel towards him as a person may be the most effective way of influencing him to examine his behavior and perhaps subsequently change it. The invariant expression of warmth seems to induce a great deal of liking, but does not influence another person to engage in behavior which you feel is more constructive. It is important to remember, however, that the expression of emotions such as anger is very frightening to many people and, according to Johnson's results, the person expressing anger tends to underestimate its alienating effect upon the listener. If you express anger in confronting another person, furthermore, it is important to pay close attention to your audience; you may be able to express anger towards a friend in ways that effectively confront his destructive behavior and lead to increased affection, but other individuals watching may be frightened and be wary of you in the future.

SKILLS INVOLVED IN CONFRONTING ANOTHER PERSON

We defined a confrontation as a deliberate attempt, originating from a desire on the part of the confronter to involve himself more deeply with the person he is confronting, to help another person examine the consequences of some aspect of his behavior. Such a confrontation may be the communication of your observation of the other person's behavior plus the impact of his behavior upon you (informational confrontation), or it may be the communication of your observation of the other's behavior plus the impact of his behavior upon you plus your interpretation of what the other person's behavior means (interpretative confrontation). The confrontation must be presented in a way that facilitates the other person's examination of the consequences of his behavior rather than causes him to defend his behavior. The skills involved in confrontation involve both the communication of your observation of the other's behavior, your reaction, and your interpretation, and a desire to increase your understanding of the other person's behavior in order to increase your involvement with him and to minimize his defensiveness. Specifically, the skills are:

1. The use of personal statements. Personal statements are discussed in Chapter 4. The hallmark of a personal statement is the pronouns, *I, me,* and *my*

2. The use of relationship statements. Relationship statements are discussed in Chapter 4. Relationship statements are those in which you express what you think or feel about the person with whom you are relating.

3. The use of behavior descriptions. Behavior descriptions are discussed in Chapter 2. A behavior description is a statement describing the visible behavior of the other person.

4. Direct description of your feelings. This is described in Chapter 5. A description of your feelings must be a personal statement and specify some kind of feeling by name, action urge, simile, or other figure of speech.

5. Understanding response. This is described in Chapters 4 and 7. It involves paraphrasing the statements made by the other person.

6. Interpretative response. This is described in Chapter 7 as well as the present chapter. To be most helpful an interpretative response should have all the characteristics described on page 162–163.

7. A perception check of the other person's feelings. This is discussed in Chapter 5. In a perception check you state what you perceive to be the feeling of the other person in order to verify that your perception is correct.

8. Constructive feedback skills. These are discussed in Chapter 2.

PRACTICING CONFRONTATIONS

The following exercise provides you with an opportunity to practice confronting another person constructively. In this confrontation you should consciously apply the six skills involved in constructive confrontations. The procedure for the exercise is as follows:

1. Form a triad. Designate one person as the confronter, another as the person being confronted, and the third as an observer. The confronter should then think back upon his relationship with the person being confronted. Find some incident which you remember where you felt the other person engaged in behavior that was destructive for himself, for you, or for another person. The more recent the incident the better. Then practice the skills involved in constructive confrontation by confronting the other person with your perception, reaction, and

interpretation of his behavior. The person being confronted should respond in an authentic way. The observer should use the first column of the "Observation Sheet" found on p. 261 to evaluate the effectiveness of the confrontation.

2. After the confrontation has ended, or after 15 minutes, whichever comes first, the observer should give the confronter feedback concerning the effectiveness of his use of skills in his confrontation. The person being confronted should express his reactions to the confronter's behavior. Be sure to mention the good points while trying to find ways to improve the effectiveness of the confronter's confrontation skills.

3. Switch roles. Then repeat Steps 1 and 2.

4. Switch roles. Then repeat Steps 1 and 2.

5. In the group as a whole, share your reactions to the exercise and your impression of what each individual learned about his behavior when he attempted to confront another person.

ROLE-PLAYING CONFRONTATIONS

The objective of this exercise is to provide you with practice in using the constructive confrontation skills in a series of role-playing situations. The procedure for the exercise is:

1. Divide into triads. Designate one person as the confronter, another as the person being confronted, and the third as an observer.

2. Take the first role-playing situation. The person being confronted plays the person described in the situation. The confronter tries to confront the other with as much authenticity and involvement as possible. The observer uses the 2nd column of the "Observation Sheet" found on p. 261 to determine the effectiveness of the use of the skills involved in constructive confrontation.

3. After the confrontation has ended, give the confronter feedback concerning how well he utilized the skills involved in constructive confrontation.

4. Switch roles; repeat Steps 2 and 3.

5. Switch roles; repeat Steps 2 and 3.

6. Discuss in the group as a whole what you learn about how you may

more effectively confront other individuals. Share your reactions to the exercise.

The role-playing situations are as follows:

1. Role play a person who often criticizes the behavior of other individuals.

2. Role play a person who is extremely shy in groups.

3. Role play a person who frequently embarrasses other individuals by his gross remarks and his bad table manners.

4. Role play a person who jokes about other people's problems.

5. Role play a person who constantly expresses a great deal of affection for everyone.

6. Role play a person who is so "nice" that he is "unreal."

RELATIONSHIP CONFRONTATIONS

This exercise provides an opportunity to use confrontation to improve the quality of your relationships. The procedure for the exercise is as follows:

1. Pick out a person with whom you have a good relationship. In the pair discuss the following issues using the skills involved in constructive confrontation:
   a. "The things you do which most block the relationship are . . ."
   b. "The things you could do to improve the relationship are . . ."

2. At the end of 15 minutes stop and pick out another person with whom you have a good relationship. Pair up and discuss the two issues in Step 1.

3. At the end of 15 minutes repeat Step 1.

4. Discuss your reactions to the exercise in the group as a whole.

GOING AROUND THE CIRCLE

This exercise provides an opportunity to practice good confrontation skills with everyone in the group. The procedure for the exercise is as follows:

1. Everyone who wishes to participate in the exercise should stand in a circle.

2. One at a time, the participants walk around the circle, stopping in front of each person. You are (1) to look directly at the person, (2) to touch him, and (3) to tell him how you feel about him and your relationship.

3. After every participant has gone around the circle, the group discuss their reactions to the exercise, what they learned about themselves and each other, and what they may do to improve their relationships with the other members of the group.

MATCHING

You may wish to check your understanding of the key definitions in this chapter by matching the following (answers on p. 169):

_____ 1. Confrontation.

_____ 2. Informational confrontation.

_____ 3. Interpretative confrontation.

a. An expression of what you think or feel about the other person.

b. Your perception of another person's behavior and its consequences and its impact upon you.

c. A deliberate attempt to help another person examine the consequences of some aspect of his behavior.

d. A statement describing the visible behavior of another person.

e. Your perception of another person's behavior, its consequences, its impact upon you, and the inferences you draw about its motives and meaning.

CHECKLIST OF SKILLS

_____ I have mastered constructively confronting other individuals.

_____ I need more work on constructively confronting other individuals.

ANSWERS

Pages 161–162:   *1: a; 2: b; 3: d, e; 4: a*
Page 168:   *1: c; 2: b; 3: e*

Reinforcing
Interpersonal Skills

chapter

10

The purpose of this book is to help you increase your interpersonal skills. Interpersonal skills do not magically appear; they are learned according to the principles of reinforcement theory. Reinforcement theory consists of a few simple procedures which have very powerful effects when put into use. The contents of this chapter will help you systematically apply reinforcement theory to build better relationships, to help other individuals increase their interpersonal skills, and to increase your own interpersonal skills.

VALUE OF REINFORCEMENT THEORY

Relationships are built because they are reinforcing to the two individuals involved. Many individuals with whom you may become involved are lonely because they have not learned the skills involved in developing fulfilling relationships; through the use of reinforcement theory you may help them increase their skills. It is inevitable that you will find yourself trying out new behaviors which need to be reinforced in order to be competently developed; the use of reinforcement theory is an important tool in increasing your skills in developing and maintaining close relationships with other individuals.

Specifically, the objectives of this chapter are:

1. To communicate the basic principles of reinforcement theory.

2. To communicate how the use of reinforcement theory can increase the quality of your relationships and the level of the interpersonal skills of other individuals and yourself.

3. To provide practice in reinforcing positive behaviors in other individuals and yourself.

When using reinforcement theory the attitude you adopt towards the other individual is of great importance. Reinforcement principles can be used to manipulate and control other individuals; they can also be used to help other individuals increase their interpersonal skills and thereby increase the feelings of happiness and sense of fulfillment in their lives. In this chapter we emphasize the use of reinforcement theory to help others and facilitate their accomplishment of their goals and strengths; the use of reinforcement theory to manipulate and control others does not produce growth and should be guarded against.

We will first focus upon the use of reinforcement theory to increase the quality of our relationships, then focus upon its use to help others develop their interpersonal skills, and finally focus upon how reinforcement theory can be used to facilitate our own skill development.

REINFORCEMENT THEORY

Reinforcement theory is based upon the simple rule that behavior is influenced by its consequences. If you say "hello" to a person you are just getting to know and receive a warm smile and a "hello" back, you are likely to repeat the behavior in the future; if you receive a blank look and silence, however, you will be less likely to repeat the behavior in the future. When we engage in behavior it is to create the consequences we want; if those desired consequences do not result, we tend not to repeat the behavior but rather to switch to a new behavior that may be more effective in the future. This means that through the control of consequences you may increase, decrease, or keep constant the frequency of another person's behavior. The procedure for the use of reinforcement theory in affecting the behavior of other individuals is: (1) specify an objective (pinpoint a behavior), (2) arrange a consequence, and (3) observe for a change in the frequency of the response.

SPECIFYING OBJECTIVES

When you initiate a relationship with another person you need to be clear concerning the objectives of your behavior. When you wish to help another person increase his interpersonal skills, you need to be clear concerning the objectives of your behavior. Without a clear understanding of your objectives you will not know (1) what you are trying to achieve, (2) how you plan to achieve it, or (3) whether or not you are successful.

A fable describes the necessity for clear objectives. Once upon a time a little wild horse decided to go out and seek his fortune. The little wild horse gathered his 12 gold coins and cantered out to find his fortune. Before he had gone very far he met a fox who asked him where he was going. "I'm seeking my fortune," replied the little wild horse proudly. "You're in luck," said the fox, "for four gold coins I will sell you these magic horseshoes which will help you get there twice as fast." The little wild horse was delighted at the idea of finding his fortune twice as fast, so he bought the magic horseshoes and ran off at twice the speed. Before long he met a wolf who asked him where he was going. After learning that the little wild horse was seeking his fortune, the wolf remarked, "You're in luck! For a small fee I will let you have this jet-propelled motorcycle so that you will be able to get there a lot faster." The little wild horse paid four gold coins for the motorcycle and went roaring off five times as fast. Soon he met a rancher who asked him where he was going. "I'm seeking my fortune," replied the little wild horse. "You're in luck," said the rancher. "If you run into my corral you'll save yourself a lot of time!" "Gee, thanks," said the little wild horse, and he zoomed into the corral there to be captured. Moral: If you're not sure where you're going, you will not know how to get there, and may not even recognize it when you do.

An *objective* is a result you want to achieve with your behavior. There are three rules to follow when specifying an objective. *The first rule is: Make the objective describe behavior that is observable and countable.* You want to formulate the objective so that someone else could count the number of times the behavior indicating the accomplishment of your objective occurs. You cannot measure the effectiveness of what you are doing unless you have a countable behavior as an objective. Specifying behavioral objectives is sometimes described as "pinpointing behavior." It is not difficult to state objectives in terms of countable behaviors, but it does take some practice. It is especially important to learn to differentiate between countable and uncountable behaviors. Which of the statements listed below clearly specify a countable behavior? (Find answers on p. 187.)

1. Sharon likes me.
2. Sally is smiling.
3. Sam has a positive self-concept.
4. Jim stops me on the street to talk to me.
5. George is depressed.

6. Jane is blinking her eyes.

7. Brenda is putting her arms around me.

8. Dave is happy.

The second rule is: Specify the desired direction of the change in behavior. You should be clear whether you want to increase, decrease, or stabilize the frequency of the pinpointed behavior. In initiating a friendship, for example, you may want to increase the number of times the other person stops to talk with you, decrease the number of times he avoids you, or stabilize the number of times you do something together.

The third rule is: If a deadman can do it, it is not behavior. Being quiet, sitting still, are "deadman" behaviors. Often individuals who specify behavior objectives to decrease specify deadman behaviors; if you focus upon increasing the frequency of desirable behaviors, you will usually avoid deadman behaviors.

Below are a series of behavior targets. Which ones are acceptable in terms of the rules stated above? (Find answers on p. 187.)

1. Increase the number of times Jane says to Janet, "I like you."

2. Increase the number of times John paraphrases George's remarks when they are discussing their personal relationships.

3. Keep constant the number of times Jim does not move when Sally walks into the room.

4. Sally smiles at Jane.

5. Increase the liking Karen feels for Ann.

In order to assess your understanding of the above material you may wish to answer the following questions (answers on p. 187):

1. What rule is reinforcement theory based upon?
    a. Behavior results in consequences.
    b. Behavior is influenced by its consequences.
    c. Behavior is an individual action.
    d. Behavior is influenced by action.

2. What does the above rule mean?
    a. Actions speak louder than words.
    b. People repeat behavior that results in desired consequences.
    c. People repeat behavior that gets results.
    d. People are easily manipulated.
    e. Actions are influenced by other people's behavior.

3. What three things, in order, make up the procedure for the use of reinforcement theory?

a. Specify an objective, observe for a change in response frequency, arrange a consequence.
b. Observe for a change in response frequency, arrange a consequence, specify an objective.
c. Arrange a consequence, specify an objective, observe for a change in response frequency.
d. Specify an objective, arrange a consequence, observe for a change in response frequency.

4. What is an objective?
   a. The results of an action or behavior.
   b. A means to an end.
   c. A result you want to achieve with your behavior.
   d. Something you object to.

5. What are three rules to follow when specifying an objective?
   a. The objective should describe behavior which is observable and countable.
   b. The objective should describe common behaviors.
   c. You should specify the desired direction of the behavior change.
   d. You should tell under what circumstances the change will take place.
   e. If a deadman can do it, it isn't behavior.
   f. Anyone but a deadman can be changed by an objective.

SHAPING BEHAVIOR

Complicated behaviors are learned in small steps. Consequently, if you want to reinforce complicated behavior patterns in another person, it is useful to analyze the behavior and divide it into small, easily identifiable behaviors that can be readily reinforced. Reinforcement can lose its impact if the behaviors being reinforced are not clear; too large a behavior pattern can confuse just what the reinforcement is for.

In addition, if you want to reinforce another person for making a friend, you could wait forever before the other person makes a friend and, therefore, receives reinforcement from you. By analyzing into small behaviors what is involved in making a friend you can encourage and shape another person's behavior into the necessary skills needed for the larger goal. You could, for example, reward the other person for initiating a conversation, making personal statements, disclosing himself, showing up at a party, or a variety of other behaviors which may lead to making a friend.

1. Divide into pairs. Think of a person with whom you would like to

develop a better relationship. Pinpoint behaviors which would indicate the accomplishment of a better relationship. Then discuss the pinpointed behaviors with each other. Help each other arrive at behavioral objectives for developing a better relationship which meet the three rules discussed above and which involve shaping your own and/or the other person's behavior. The behavioral objectives you wish to accomplish with this person are:

_____

_____

_____

_____

_____

_____

Please answer the following question (answer on p. 187):

Why is it important to reinforce several small behaviors rather than a large behavior pattern? (Give two reasons.)
a. Large behavior patterns can confuse what the reinforcement is for.
b. Small behaviors are more meaningful behaviors.
c. Small behaviors are easier to reinforce.
d. Large behavior patterns may not occur often enough to reinforce.

ARRANGE A CONSEQUENCE

The two major types of consequences that you may use to change the frequency of a pinpointed behavior are: (1) strengthening consequences such as warmth and acceptance, and (2) weakening consequences such as coolness and ignoring. These two types of consequences may be used to increase, decrease, or maintain the frequency of a behavior of another person.

To increase the frequency of a behavior of another person, it is important that you (1) give it a strengthening consequence, (2) immediately, and (3) consistently. The more immediate the strengthening consequence follows the behavior it is aimed at reinforcing, the more reinforcing it will be; too long a delay between the pinpointed behavior and the strengthening consequence can lead to a misunderstanding causing other behaviors than the pinpointed behavior to be strengthened. If, for example, a person initiates a conversation, is ignored, leaves, and then is given approval for the initiation attempt, what may actually be reinforced is his tendency to leave whenever an attempt to establish contact with another person fails.

Correspondingly, when the frequency of a behavior is being increased, it is important that the person receive a strengthening consequence consistently every time he engages in the behavior. Only if the strengthening consequence is received consistently will a person increase the frequency of the behavior during a short time period.

There are two approaches to decreasing the frequency of a behavior of another person. The first is (1) to give a weakening consequence, (2) immediately, and (3) consistently. The second is to increase the frequency of an incompatible behavior. Increasing the frequency of an incompatible behavior is usually preferred in this situation. If, for example, a person talks too much when he first meets another person, you can begin reinforcing him for probing statements to draw the other person out and attentively listening to what the other person has to say. Or, if a person does not talk enough when he first meets another person, you can give strengthening consequences for his talking about himself.

If you wish to maintain the frequency of a behavior of another person, it is important that you (1) give a strengthening consequence, (2) immediately, and (3) inconsistently. While consistency is important for increasing the frequency of a behavior, it is better to present strengthening consequences less consistently in order to maintain the behavior at a certain level. When you switch from presenting the strengthening consequence consistently to inconsistently, change gradually; do not change the frequency suddenly.

How do you tell what is a strengthening consequence for another individual? The expression of acceptance and warmth is commonly accepted as a strengthening consequence; in addition, there are times when the various responses such as the understanding response are strengthening consequences through communicating interest and concern. Ignoring the behavior of the other person is commonly accepted as a weakening response. By observing the other person and by asking the other person what it is that he values from other people, it is possible to find out what consequences the other person feels are strengthening or weakening. It is important to remember that there are large individual differences; what is strengthening for you may not be strengthening for another person.

2. At this point divide into pairs again. Think of behaviors that you could engage in that are strengthening or weakening consequences for the person you wish to develop a better relationship with. What could you do that would strengthen the behavior of the other person? Discuss your answer with your partner. Help each other specify as precisely as possible the consequences that would strengthen the pin-

pointed behavior of the person you wish to develop a better relation-ship with. The behavior that you could engage in that would serve as a strengthening consequence for the pinpointed behavior of the other person is:

_____

_____

_____

_____

_____

Please answer the following questions (answers on p. 187):

1. What are the three steps for increasing the frequency of behavior?
   a. Give a strengthening consequence.
   b. Give a weakening consequence.
   c. Give no consequence.
   d. Immediately.
   e. Later.
   f. Consistently.
   g. Inconsistently.

2. What are the three steps for decreasing the frequency of behavior?
   a. Give a strengthening consequence.
   b. Give a weakening consequence.
   c. Give no consequence.
   d. Immediately.
   e. Later.
   f. Consistently.
   g. Inconsistently.

3. What are the three steps for maintaining the frequency of behavior?
   a. Give a strengthening consequence.
   b. Give a weakening consequence.
   c. Give no consequence.
   d. Immediately.
   e. Later.
   f. Consistently.
   g. Inconsistently.

4. What are usually two strengthening consequences?
   a. Expression of warmth and acceptance.
   b. Expression of coldness.

    c. Understanding response.

    d. Ignoring behavior.

5. What are usually two weakening consequences?

    a. Expression of warmth and acceptance.

    b. Expression of coldness.

    c. Understanding response.

    d. Ignoring behavior.

OBSERVING FOR A CHANGE IN THE OTHER'S BEHAVIOR

The conscientious reader will profit a great deal by keeping records of the number of times the person he is building a relationship with engages in the pinpointed behavior. It is quite common for people to completely misjudge the frequency of another person's behavior. Also, it is quite common for people to completely misjudge the effect of the consequences they provide for other people's behavior. The classic example is the teacher who pays attention to a disruptive student in order to tell him to behave himself. Constant reminders to behave oneself often *increase* the amount of disruptive behavior a student engages in. It is, however, only after records of the student's behavior are being kept that the teacher discovers this. The critical importance of clearly specifying behavioral objectives is to be able to count the number of times the other person engages in the behavior in order to determine whether your behavior is having the intended effect upon the other person's behavior.

Divide into pairs. Help each other plan ways of counting the number of times the individual you wish to develop a better relationship with engages in the specified behavior. During the next week observe carefully and report the results back to the group.

REINFORCING THE OTHER'S STRENGTHS

Many people have very few close friends merely because they have never developed the skills necessary to build close friendships. Many people who find themselves without close friends are the victims of circumstances that have placed them in few situations in which to develop effective relationship skills. Many people have not learned the skills of initiating and maintaining rewarding relationships with others. In initiating friendships with other individuals, you may become involved with such a person. In such a case, you may wish to apply reinforcement theory to help a person who has low interpersonal skills to become more skillful in relating to other people.

In addition to individuals who have never had an opportunity to develop effective interpersonal skills, we all know individuals who have many strengths and who could be quite skillful interpersonally but who have barriers such as feelings of insecurity and lack of self-confidence that block them from developing the number of close friendships they otherwise could have. There are real risks to a person's feelings of self-worth involved in reaching out to other individuals and initiating relationships; when such an attempt is rejected, it commonly results in hurt feelings. Whether a person is able to take such risks may depend upon his level of self-confidence and self-acceptance and the expression of support he receives from his current friends. When one of your friends is blocked by a lack of self-confidence or a fear of rejection from increasing his interpersonal skills or building more fulfilling relationships, you may wish to apply the principles of reinforcement theory to provide the support and encourage the feelings of self-confidence he needs.

Being a person's friend means that you should be supportive. Being supportive can be defined as communicating to another person that you recognize his strengths and believe he has the capabilities of handling productively whatever situation he faces. Becoming involved with a person who in your judgment has few interpersonal skills entails the responsibility of helping that person increase his interpersonal effectiveness. When a friend does not have the self-confidence to risk initiating closer relationships with others, you may be able to provide support in ways which increase his self-confidence and self-acceptance so that he is free to take such risks in the future. How do you do all these things? What are the procedures for being supportive and helpful to other people? Reinforcement theory helps answer these questions.

Everyone builds upon his strengths. Feeling confidence in your strengths is vital to the self-acceptance needed to risk trying out new behaviors in order to build better interpersonal skills. As an individual becomes more aware of his strengths and more confident in his ability to demonstrate his strengths he will gain the self-confidence needed to develop increased interpersonal skills and build better relationships. The way in which reinforcement theory is helpful in providing support and encouraging constructive behaviors is, therefore, in giving strengthening consequences immediately after the person has engaged in a behavior that demonstrates one of these strengths or indicates an attempt to overcome a barrier to the expression of his strengths.

Please answer the following question (answer on p. 187):

What does being supportive to another person involve?

a. Communicating that you recognize his strengths and believe that he can handle any situation productively.

b. Communicating that you recognize his strengths and will help him with his weaknesses.
c. Communicating that you recognize his strengths and will help him compensate for his weaknesses.
d. Communicating that you recognize his strengths and don't see his weaknesses.

EXERCISE IN REINFORCING ANOTHER PERSON'S STRENGTHS

The objective of the following exercise is to provide practice in reinforcing another person for engaging in behaviors that demonstrate one of his basic strengths or attempt to overcome a barrier to the expression of his strengths. The procedure for the exercise is as follows:

1. Think of a person you know (1) whom you could help improve his relationship skills, (2) who lacks the self-confidence to utilize his relationship skills, or (3) whom you would like to express more support to. In the space below, describe this person's basic strengths.

_____

_____

_____

_____

_____

_____

2. What are the barriers which keep this person from expressing his strengths in interpersonal situations? Examples of possible barriers are a lack of self-confidence, fear of rejection, fear that friends will think he is foolish, wanting to be overly nice, or lack of self-acceptance.
   The barriers for this person are:

_____

_____

_____

_____

_____

_____

3. What are the possible strengthening consequences for this person you could provide? Examples of possible strengthening consequences are the expression of warmth, acceptance, encouragement, understanding, self-disclosure about your positive reactions to his behavior, and many of the other behaviors that have been discussed in this book.

The behaviors which you could engage in that are possible strengthening consequences are:

_____

_____

_____

_____

_____

4. Reviewing what you have listed in Steps 1, 2, and 3, write out a series of behavioral objectives for your interactions with the person for the following week. Such a list should include a statement of countable behavior on the part of the other person, directionality of change in the countable behavior, and a description of countable behavior by you to provide a strengthening consequence. An example of such a behavioral objective is, "increase the number of times John initiates a conversation by expressing warmth towards him immediately after he does so in my presence."

My objectives are:

_____

_____

_____

_____

_____

5. Review your objectives. It is important that they are not attempts to manipulate the other person, but rather expressions of support for behaviors you feel will facilitate the person's expression of his strengths or the elimination of barriers to the demonstration of his strengths. Your objectives should reflect a sincere attempt to be supportive, not an attempt to remake the other person. On the basis of your review, rewrite any objectives which may seem more manipulative than supportive.

6. In the group as a whole, discuss the objectives you have listed. Review what you wrote on Steps 1, 2, and 3 in order to provide background for the objectives written in Step 4. Help each other increase the specificity and concreteness of your objectives. Suggest new ideas for strengthening consequences for each other; help each other write new objectives that may be more effective in helping the other person.

7. During the next week, keep the "Record Sheet" found on p. 263. Bring the sheet back to the group meeting and discuss the results. Is there any relationship between the number of strengthening consequences you engaged in and the number of times the other person engaged in behaviors which demonstrated his strengths or attempts to overcome barriers to the expression of his strengths?

EXERCISE IN REINFORCING YOUR OWN STRENGTHS

In addition to reinforcing another person's strengths, you can set up situations in which your own behavior gets reinforced. Through such reinforcement systems you may maximize your strengths and facilitate the development of your interpersonal skills. The process is the same as reinforcing another person's behavior; when your behavior is followed by a strengthening consequence, you will tend to repeat the behavior. The more immediately the strengthening consequence follows your behavior, the more likely you will be to repeat the behavior in the future. If you consistently receive a strengthening consequence immediately after engaging in the behavior, you will increase the number of times you engage in the behavior at a rapid rate; to maintain the frequency of your behavior it is better to receive strengthening consequences immediately, but inconsistently. When you have important goals you are trying to accomplish, it is often helpful to find ways of receiving reinforcers for engaging in the behavior that will facilitate the accomplishment of your goal.

In this book are discussed a variety of interpersonal skills that will increase the quality of your relationship if put to use. But in order to apply what is learned you need to have some personal goals concerning the building of better relationships, apply the skills in a systematic way, and build systems to receive reinforcement for engaging in the skills. Such a process involves being aware of, and building upon, your present strengths and skills. This does not mean you cannot develop new strengths; indeed, the purpose of this book is to help you develop new strengths in interpersonal skills. But developing new strengths is facilitated by being aware of and using your present strengths.

The objective of this exercise is to provide you with an opportunity to use reinforcement theory to increase the number or quality of your strengths in relating to other individuals. The procedure for the exercise is as follows:

1. Set a goal for using the skills presented in the previous chapters of this book in increasing the quality of your relationship with one or more individuals. The goal is:

_____

_____

_____

_____

_____

2. What specific behaviors will you have to engage in to accomplish your goal? What specific behaviors will indicate that the goal is accomplished?

_____

_____

_____

_____

_____

3. What personal strengths will you utilize to accomplish your goal?

_____

_____

_____

_____

_____

4. What are the barriers to your using your strengths to accomplish your goal?

_____

_____

_____

_____

_____

_____

5. Review what you have written for Steps 1, 2, 3, and 4. Set a series of behavioral objectives for yourself. Make sure that they are countable and have direction.

_____

_____

_____

_____

_____

6. In the group as a whole, review each person's objectives. Set aside some time during the next several group meetings to review each member's progress towards accomplishing his objectives. All possible support should be given to the members of the group who make progress towards achieving their objectives. It is the support and praise of the group that will serve as the major strengthening consequence for engaging in the behavior that facilitates the accomplishment of your objectives.

SUMMARY QUESTIONNAIRE

1. My long-term objectives for building better relationships are:

_____

_____

_____

2. My short-term objectives for building better relationships are:

_____

_____

_____

_____

3. The strengths and skills I will use to accomplish my objectives are:

_____

_____

_____

_____

4. The way in which I will know when my objectives are accomplished is:

_____

_____

_____

_____

5. The system of reinforcement for the behavior I engage in to accomplish my objectives is:

_____

_____

_____

_____

CHECKLIST OF SKILLS

1. I can reinforce behaviors in other people in order to:

    _____ Increase the frequency of behavior.

    _____ Decrease the frequency of behavior.

    _____ Maintain the frequency of behavior.

2. I can arrange for my behavior to be reinforced in order to:

    _____ Increase the number or quality of my strengths.

    _____ Decrease the number of self-defeating behaviors.

    _____ Maintain the frequency of effective behaviors.

3. I need more work on:

    _____ Reinforcing other people's behavior.

    _____ Arranging reinforcements for my behavior.

ANSWERS

Pages 173–174: 2, 4, 6, 7
Page 174: 1, 2
Pages 174–175: 1: b; 2: b; 3: d; 4: c; 5: a, c, e
Page 176: a, d
Pages 178–179: 1: a, d, f; 2: b, d, f; 3: a, d, g; 4: a, c; 5: b, d
Pages 180–181: a

Modeling
Interpersonal Skills

chapter **11**

When you become involved with a person who has never learned many effective interpersonal skills you may wish to help him do so. In the previous chapter we emphasized that behavior is influenced by its consequences and, through the control of consequences, you could increase the number of times another individual engaged in constructive behavior by providing strengthening consequences. Another way to help a person increase his interpersonal skills is to model behavior to be imitated by that person. Modeling interpersonal skills becomes a primary means of helping others acquire more effective behaviors. It is for this reason that we discuss modeling in this chapter. Specifically, the objectives of this chapter are:

1. To explain modeling theory.
2. To provide an experience in which you may practice modeling effective interpersonal skills.

MODELING THEORY

The word *modeling* refers to the process by which one person engages in ideal behavior to serve as an example to be imitated by other persons. If you, for example, engage in self-disclosure and another person imitates you by also engaging in self-disclosure, a modeling process has taken place. The saying, "Don't do as I do, do as I say," recognizes that sometimes other persons learn more from imitating us than we would like them to. Learning new behaviors by imitating others is a major means of acquiring new skills. People who have never learned the skills necessary to initiate, develop, and maintain effective interpersonal relationships can learn many of the behaviors involved just by imitating a person who demonstrates them.

There are three major ways in which a person who is relatively unskilled in interpersonal relations may benefit from observing you model effective interpersonal skills. The first is by acquiring new skills he did not previously have by imitating you. If he does not know how to initiate a relationship, observing you doing so will help him learn.

The second is by seeing you receive a strengthening consequence for your behavior; thus he will be more likely to engage in the same behavior. This is perhaps the most influential aspect of modeling. If a person sees you receive an immediate strengthening consequence after engaging in the behavior, he will be likely to imitate it. Or, if he sees you as being prestigious, competent, or having power, he will tend to imitate your behavior. Finally, a person's fears, anxieties, and inhibitions about engaging in the behavior can be reduced by observing you engage in the behavior; if he is fearful of rejection, for example, observing you initiate a conversation with another person without being rejected will reduce his fear.

The third way in which a relatively unskilled person may benefit from observing you model effective interpersonal behavior is by having the same behavior elicited or triggered in himself. Many times the other person has the appropriate skills but may not be sure of when and where they should be used; seeing you engage in the behavior, he learns that the current situation is one in which the behaviors are appropriate.

There are two steps to the modeling process: first, you have to engage in the ideal behavior; second, the other person has to imitate you. The first is entirely under your control, but the second is primarily under the control of the other person. How do you influence another person to imitate the behavior you are modeling? What are the circumstances under which he will do so?

First, the other person must pay attention to what you are doing; if the other person is not aware of your behavior, he cannot imitate it. Second, if the person thinks that imitating your behavior will help him accomplish his goals, he will be more likely to do so, especially if he feels deprived of the goals at the moment. For example, if the person's goals are to increase the number of his friends and he feels lonely, he will imitate your behavior if he perceives it as relevant to making more friends. Third, if imitating your behavior has proved helpful in the past, the person will be more likely to imitate you in the present. Fourth, the more the person values your friendship, likes you, looks up to you, or

seeks your approval, the more likely it is that he will imitate your behavior. Fifth, if the person is emotionally aroused, such as being lonely
or feeling lots of warmth, he will tend to imitate your behavior more than
if he is not emotionally aroused. Finally, if the person does not know
what behavior is appropriate in the situation and you do, he will tend to
imitate you (the classic example is the person who finds himself at a
formal dinner without knowing the order in which he is supposed to
use the silverware—he will watch to see what piece of silverware the other
people pick up first and imitate them).

If you want to help other people develop the skills necessary for initiating, developing, and maintaining friendships you must demonstrate the
skills yourself. You must behave the way you want other people to behave. Thus it is important for you to model effective behavior in order
to help other persons increase their skills in building fulfilling relationships.

You may wish to assess your understanding of the material in this section by answering the following questions (answers on p. 193):

1. What is "modeling"?
   a. Showing off your skills in interpersonal relationships.
   b. Engaging in ideal behavior to be imitated by others.
   c. Applying reinforcement theory.
   d. Showing off new clothes.

2. What are three ways by which an unskilled person may benefit from
   observing your modeling of effective interpersonal skills?
   a. By seeing you being reinforced for your behavior.
   b. By being reinforced by you for his behavior.
   c. By imitating you.
   d. By helping him plan how to demonstrate interpersonal skills.
   e. By triggering the behavior in him.

3. Under what three conditions will a person imitate your behavior?
   a. If imitating your behavior has been helpful in the past.
   b. If he is good at imitation.
   c. If it will help him accomplish his goals.
   d. If he has been unsuccessful with other methods.
   e. If he is aware of your behavior.
   f. If you tell him to do it.

EXERCISE IN MODELING EFFECTIVE INTERPERSONAL SKILLS

This exercise provides an opportunity to practice the skills discussed in
the previous chapters in order that you may effectively model them. The
following is a list of the skills.

1. Self-disclosure.
2. Behavior-description.
3. Personal statements.
4. Relationship statements.
5. Direct description of feelings.
6. Nonverbal expression of warmth and liking.
7. Giving constructive feedback.
8. Perception check of other's feelings.
9. Confirming the other's strengths.
10. Reinforcing the other's strengths.
11. Expressing acceptance of the other person and his behavior.
12. Understanding response.
13. Negotiating for meaning response.
14. Evaluative response.
15. Interpretative response.
16. Supportive response.
17. Probing response.
18. Confronting the other person.
19. Building trust.

The procedure for the exercise is as follows:

1. Review the list of skills presented above; make sure you are familiar with each one.
2. Divide into groups of four. Discuss the problems you are having in applying the skills you are learning from this book to your personal relationships. *During this discussion consciously try to model as many of the above skills as possible.*
3. Divide into new groups of four. Discuss the ways in which applying the skills you are learning from this book has helped you in relating to other people. *During this discussion consciously try to model as many of the above skills as possible.*
4. In the group as a whole discuss:
   a. What are the problems you experience in trying to model the skills discussed in this book?
   b. How may you more effectively model the skills discussed in this book in the presence of persons you are building a relationship with?

5. Think of one of your relationships. In this relationship, plan how to model at least three of the above skills during the next week.

CHECKLIST OF SKILLS

1. I can effectively model the following skills:

_____ Self-disclosure.

_____ Behavior-description.

_____ Personal statements.

Relationship statements.

_____ Direct description of feelings.

_____ Nonverbal expression of warmth and liking.

_____ Giving constructive feedback.

_____ Perception check of other's feelings.

_____ Confirming the other's strengths.

_____ Reinforcing the other's strengths.

_____ Expressing acceptance of the other person and his behavior.

_____ Understanding response.

_____ Negotiating for meaning response.

_____ Evalautive response.

_____ Interpretative response.

_____ Supportive response.

_____ Probing response.

_____ Confronting the other person.

_____ Building trust.

ANSWERS

Page 191:   *1: b; 2: a, c, e; 3: a, c, e*

Solving
Interpersonal Problems

chapter **12**

In any relationship there are times when problems arise. These problems may be conflicts, periods of irritation, or periods where the relationship is changing and you are unsure of where it is going. In this chapter we will focus upon a way to analyze interpersonal problems to facilitate their solution. Specifically, the objective of the chapter, much of it adapted from an exercise by Saul Eisen, is to present a programmed approach to defining an interpersonal problem and planning for its solution.

SOLVING INTERPERSONAL PROBLEMS

Individuals who are most successful at resolving personal problems typically go through certain general stages of thinking about their problems. At each stage they find a new, more useful way of looking at the problem in order to obtain a better understanding of it and to help them uncover new approaches for solving it. This chapter will present a systematic procedure for thinking about a problem you now have with another person in order to help you understand the problem and plan how to solve it.

Choose a problem you are now having in relating to another person. Be sure that the problem meets the following criteria:

1. It is important to you.
2. You are personally involved.

3. You really want to solve it.

4. It is solvable.

You will now be asked a series of questions about the way you think about your problem. As you answer these questions you will be following a process that results in more effective ways of looking at your problem. You will be going through the stages of effective problem solving. In the following steps you will be asked to write down a simple statement of your problem. This first statement will probably not be very clear or concise. In fact, part of the difficulty in solving a problem is that often it is hard to pin down just what the problem is. This chapter will help you to state your problem more clearly.

Take some time to write down the first statement of your problem as it looks to you now. You need not worry about how clear the statement of your problem is, or how well you have written it; try instead to write it "off the top of your head."

As I see the problem, it is essential that:

_____

_____

_____

_____

_____

_____

_____

_____

Now that you have written down how the problem looks at this point, it would be helpful to see what stage of problem-solving your statement represents. If you think about the problem as something that is bad in general but has no bearing on you personally, you are thinking in Stage One; if you think about how it involves *you*, you are thinking in Stage Two (see table following).

Stage One	*Stage Two*
My friend loses his temper too easily.	My friend loses his temper at me too easily.

Looking at the words you have actually written for the definition of your problem, decide whether you were thinking in Stage One or Stage Two.

For the most part, my statement is now in Stage _____.

If it is in Stage One, answer the next question. If it is in Stage Two, scan the next question, answer it if you wish, and then go on to the following paragraph.

If your problem is stated in Stage One, it did not describe the problem as *your* problem. You can progress to Stage Two by restating the problem in terms of how you are involved in it. You can do this by answering the question, "How is this a problem to *me*?" or "How am *I* concerned with it?"

If I were to redefine the problem, this time emphasizing how it involves *me*, I would say that

_____

_____

_____

_____

_____

_____

Now look again at the problem as you formulate it. If you discuss how the problem is of concern to you, but not about how you *feel* and *react* in the problem situation, you're thinking in Stage Two; but if you *also* talk about your feelings and reactions, you're thinking in Stage Three (see table following)

Stage Two	*Stage Three*
My friend gets angry at me too easily.	My friend gets angry at me too easily. This usually gets me rattled so I can't concentrate on what I am doing or have any fun, and it gets me annoyed at him for having such a short temper.

For the most part, my statement of the problem is now in Stage

_____.

If your statement of the problem is in Stage Two, go to the next paragraph. If it is in Stage Three, scan the next paragraph, answer the question if you wish, and then proceed to the following paragraph.

In order to phrase your problem in Stage Three, write it again, this time emphasizing how you *feel* and *react* in the problem situation.

Focusing now on my feelings and reactions, I would say that

_____

_____

_____

_____

_____

_____

_____

Stage Four, which is one of the crucial stages in understanding and resolving a problem, is the recognition of your "contribution"—the ways in which your behavior adds to the problem situation. If your statement includes recognition of how you help create or continue your problem, then you are at Stage Four (see table following).

Stage Three	*Stage Four*
My friend gets angry at me too easily. This usually gets me rattled so I can't concentrate on what I am doing or have any fun, and it gets me annoyed at him for having such a short temper.	My friend gets angry at me too easily. This usually gets me so rattled I can't concentrate on what I am doing or have any fun, and it gets me annoyed at him for having such a short temper. My feelings about his anger keep me on edge so that I am more likely to make the mistakes that get him angry. Also, he doesn't know the effect his anger has upon me because I've never directly informed him.

Looking at your present statement of the problem, ask yourself whether

you have fully explored your contribution to the problem in terms of the things you do or neglect to do that may be adding to it. If you've already done this, scan the next paragraph, answer the question if you wish, and then go on to the following paragraph. If you haven't, proceed to the next paragraph.

State your problem in Stage Four: The problem as I see it now, including recognizing my contribution to the problem through things I am doing or neglecting to do, is as follows:

_____

_____

_____

_____

_____

_____

_____

When you have gone through Stages One to Four in thinking about your problem you may find that you now have a clearer, more useful way of perceiving it. You may also find that some of your feelings about the situation have changed or are beginning to change. This could mean that negative, uncomfortable feelings are becoming less intense or less upsetting.

Think for a few minutes about changes in your awareness and feelings about your problem situation that have taken place as a result of analyzing it.

The following changes in my understanding of and my feelings about my problem as a result of analyzing it have taken (or are taking) place:

_____

_____

_____

_____

_____

_____

_____

Now examine the following list of skills discussed in this book. Check the skills that would be helpful for solving your problem if you would engage in the necessary behaviors.

_____ 1. Self-disclosure.

_____ 2. Behavior-description.

_____ 3. Personal statements.

_____ 4. Relationship statements.

_____ 5. Direct description of your feelings.

_____ 6. Nonverbal expression of warmth and liking.

_____ 7. Giving the other person helpful feedback.

_____ 8. Perception check of the other's feelings.

_____ 9. Confirming the other's strengths.

_____ 10. Reinforcing the other's strengths.

_____ 11. Expressing acceptance of the other person.

_____ 12. Understanding response.

_____ 13. Negotiating for meaning response.

_____ 14. Evaluative response.

_____ 15. Interpretative response.

_____ 16. Supportive response.

_____ 17. Probing response.

_____ 18. Confronting the other person.

_____ 19. Building trust.

_____ 20. Modeling ideal behavior.

List the strengths that you have which you might put into operation in order to solve the problem.

1. _____

2. _____

3. _____

4. _____

5. _____

6. _____

Think for a few minutes about specific changes in your behavior which might be helpful in solving your problem. Then complete the following.

In relation to the problem I've described and any changes in understanding of and feelings about the problem which I'm experiencing, the following specific changes in my behavior would be helpful in solving the problem:

_____

_____

_____

_____

_____

_____

In preparation for trying out the changes in behavior that you have described above, review and picture them in your imagination. How willing are you actually to try out these behavior changes? How would you rate your willingness to try out your behavior changes on the following scale?

Not willing at all 1 : 2 : 3 : 4 : 5 : 6 : 7 : 8 : 9 Completely willing

Remember, the solution to your problem depends, at least in part, on *your* behavior, *your* feelings, *your* attitudes, and *your* willingness to change.

This concludes the planning process for solving your problem. If the problem situation does not seem completely resolved after you engage in the above behaviors, or if you are now facing other problems, you may go through the planning process again in an attempt to describe your problem and the alternative behaviors for solving it more fully.

Resolving
Interpersonal Conflicts

chapter

13

Every relationship contains elements of conflict, disagreement, and opposed interests. An *interpersonal conflict* exists whenever an action by one person prevents, obstructs, or interferes with the actions of another person; there can be conflicts between goals, ways of accomplishing the same goal, personal needs, and expectations concerning the behavior of the two individuals. It is inevitable that you will become involved in conflicts whenever you have a relationship with another person. A conflict-free relationship may only be a sign that you really have no relationship at all, not that you have a good relationship. The number of conflicts you and the other person have will vary from relationship to relationship, but even in the most friendly relationships conflicts appear at times.

HANDLING OF CONFLICTS

Despite the inevitability of interpersonal conflicts, there seems to be a general feeling in our society that conflicts are bad and should be avoided and that a good relationship is one in which there are no conflicts. Many discussions of conflict cast it in the role of causing divorces, separations, psychological distress, social disorder, and even violence. There is a growing recognition, however, that it is failure to handle conflicts in constructive ways that leads to the destruction of relationships, not the mere presence of conflict. It is through the resolution of conflicts that most constructive problem-solving is initiated; when conflict is handled constructively it can lead to increased closeness and a higher quality of relationship. Many individuals seek out conflicts through such activities as competitive sports and games, movies, plays, books, and teasing. Conflicts are often of personal value leading to personal change, growth, creativeness, and curiosity. Learning how to manage your conflicts constructively may lead to increased self-confidence, greater willingness to take risks in increasing the quality of your relationships, and greater ability to handle stress and difficulty.

Since conflict is a pervasive and inevitable part of your relationships and potentially leads to your growth and development as an individual, it becomes important for you to learn the skills involved in handling conflicts constructively. If you are concerned with avoiding conflicts, resolving them prematurely, or stifling any discussion of differences, this can lead to serious difficulties within a relationship. Until a relationship is able to withstand the stress involved in a conflict, it is not likely that it will last very long. The objectives of this chapter, therefore, are:

1. To communicate how conflicts may be managed in constructive ways.
2. To provide some practice and experiences in constructively managing interpersonal conflicts.

You may wish to determine how well you understand the material in this section by answering the following questions (answers on p. 225):

1. An interpersonal conflict exists whenever:
   a. One person meets another person.
   b. Several people are trying to relate to each other.
   c. An action by one person interferes with the actions of someone else.
   d. An action by one person interferes with his best interests.
2. A good relationship is one in which:
   a. There are no conflicts.
   b. There are many conflicts.
   c. Conflicts are dealt with constructively.
   d. Conflicts are diverted into other activities.
3. Learning to manage conflicts leads to which three of the following:
   a. Increased number of friends.
   b. Increased self-confidence.
   c. Greater ability to handle stress and difficulty.
   d. Greater tolerance for others.
   e. Greater willingness to take risks in increasing the quality of your relationships.
   f. Longer life.
   g. The leading role in the school play.

YOUR STYLE OF CONFLICT MANAGEMENT

In learning how to handle conflicts constructively, the first step is to become more aware of your present and past style of managing conflict. Think back over the interpersonal conflicts you have been involved in during the past few years. These conflicts may be with friends, parents, brothers and sisters, girl friends or boy friends, husbands or wives, teachers or students, or with your boss or subordinates. In the spaces following, list the five major conflicts you can remember and how you resolved them. Since the space is limited, you may wish to abbreviate by writing down only the key words that describe your style of conflict management and the conflict situations you have been involved in.

My Conflicts	*How I Resolved the Conflict*

My Conflicts	*How I Resolved the Conflict*

DIVISION OF MONEY EXERCISE

The objective of this exercise is to place you in a conflict situation so that you can examine your present style of dealing with conflicts. The procedure for the exercise is as follows:

1. Divide into triads. Each person contributes 25 cents to the triad. The 75 cents should be placed in the middle of the triad.

2. The triad has 15 minutes to decide how to divide the money between two individuals. Only two individuals can receive money. It is not legitimate to use any sort of "chance" procedure, such as drawing straws or flipping a coin, to decide which two persons get what amounts of money. You must negotiate within the triad to reach a decision. *The purpose of the exercise is to get as much money for yourself as possible.*

3. As soon as your triad reaches a decision, write out your answers to the following questions:
   a. What were your feelings during the exercise? Be as specific and descriptive as possible.

_____

_____

b. What behaviors did you engage in during the exercise? Be as specific and descriptive as possible.

_____

_____ .

_____

_____

c. How would you characterize your style of resolving the conflict in this exercise? Be as specific and descriptive as possible.

_____

_____

_____

_____

4. In your triad, give each other feedback concerning what you perceived to be the feelings, behaviors, and conflict styles of each other.
5. In the group as a whole, describe what you learned about yourself and your style of dealing with conflicts.

EXERCISE ON GIVING AND TAKING

Many individuals find that it is easier for them to give than to receive or easier for them to have things taken from them than to take from others. In dealing with conflicts, the ability to receive and to take from others in order to maximize your own gains are as important as being willing to give to others and to let others take from you. The objective of the following exercise is to increase your awareness of your feelings and behavior in a situation involving (1) giving and receiving and (2) taking and being taken from. The procedure for the exercise is as follows:

1. The group sits in a circle. Each person takes all his coins from his pocket or purse and places them in front of him.
2. For five minutes each person gives away as little or as much of his change as he wishes to as many or few members of the group as he chooses. What you give away is for keeps. Take your time in deciding just what you want to do. You can begin passing out money whenever you feel like it.

3. Answer the following questions:
   a. Describe as specifically as possible your behavior during this part of the exercise.

   _____

   _____

   _____

   _____

   b. Describe as specifically as possible your feelings about giving your money to other persons and to receiving money from other persons.

   _____

   _____

   _____

   _____

4. Discuss as a group the reactions the members had to giving and receiving money. Describe your impressions of the other members during this part of the exercise. *Keep all your present coins in front of you.*

5. For five minutes each person takes as much or as little money as he wishes from as few or as many persons as he chooses. You are free to help yourself *for keeps* to as much money as you wish from whomever you wish in the group.

6. Answer the following:
   a. Describe as specifically as possible your behavior during this part of the exercise.

   _____

   _____

   _____

   b. Describe as specifically as possible your feelings about taking money from others and having others take money from you.

   _____

   _____

   _____

   _____

7. Discuss as a group the reactions of the members to taking money and having money taken from them. Describe your impressions of each

other during this part of the exercise. Any money you now have is yours for keeps.

NONVERBAL CONFLICT EXERCISES

Before you begin these exercises please review the discussion of nonverbal exercises in Chapter 3. A number of nonverbal exercises dealing with various aspects of conflicts may be helpful in clarifying your feelings about conflict and your style of managing conflicts. The exercises are as follows:

1. *Pushing and shoving:* Two people lock fingers, with arms extended over their heads. Push against each other, trying to drive one person to the wall.

2. *Thumb wrestling:* Lock fingers with another person with your thumbs straight up. Tap your thumbs together three times and then each person tries to pin the other's thumb so that the other cannot move it.

3. *Slapping hands:* Person *A* puts his hands out, palms down. Person *B* extends his hands, palms up, under Person *A*'s hands. The object of the exercise is for Person *B* to try to slap the hands of Person *A* by quickly moving his hands from the bottom to the top. As soon as Person *B* makes a move, Person *A* tries to pull his hands out of the way before Person *B* can slap them.

4. *Pushing down to the floor and helping up:* In pairs, one person tries to push the other person down to the floor. No wrestling, but the person being pushed may resist if he wants to. After the person is pushed down to the floor, then the pusher has to help the pushed person up. The person being helped up may still resist if he wants to.

5. *Unwrapping:* A member who is having internal conflicts is asked to make himself into a tight ball. Another person is chosen by him to "unwrap" him, or to open him up completely. The member may struggle against being unwrapped, or he may submit. Other members of the group may join in, some trying to keep the person wrapped and others trying to unwrap him. Or everyone in the group may pair up and take turns being unwrapped and unwrapping.

SUMMARY

In the space following, describe what you have learned about your style of conflict management from the above exercises:

_____

_____

_____

_____

_____

_____

_____

_____

_____

_____

_____

_____

DIMENSIONS OF CONFLICT SITUATIONS

In our discussion of managing conflicts constructively, we will focus upon several dimensions of conflict situations: obtaining an accurate perception of the conflict, ensuring accurate communication, building a climate of trust, structuring cooperative resolutions, and defining the conflict.

ACCURATE PERCEPTION OF ONE'S AND ANOTHER'S BEHAVIOR

In conflict situations there are often perceptual distortions concerning your own and the other person's behavior, motivations, and position. Many of these distortions in perception are so common that they can be found in almost any conflict situation, whether it is between two individuals, two groups, or two countries. They are:

1. *Mirror image:* It is not uncommon for both you and the other person to feel that you are an innocent victim who represents truth and justice and who is being attacked maliciously by an evil enemy. In most conflicts, both parties are firmly convinced that they are right and the

other person is wrong, that they want a "just" solution but the other party doesn't.

2. *Mote-beam mechanism:* Often in conflict situations each party clearly perceives all the underhanded and vicious acts of the other party while being completely blind to identical acts engaged in by oneself. In most conflicts both parties repress all awareness of the mean things they do to the other person but become quite indignant about the mean things the other person does to them.

3. *Double standard:* Even if both parties are aware of identical acts engaged in by themselves and the other person, there is a strong tendency to feel that what is legitimate for you to do is illegitimate for the other person to do.

4. *Polarized thinking:* It is common in conflict situations for both individuals to have an oversimplified view of the conflict in which everything they do is good and everything the other does is bad.

Such misunderstandings escalate the conflict and make it more difficult to resolve it constructively. As long as you and the other person are convinced that you are right and the other person is wrong, perceive every underhanded thing the other person does but ignore every underhanded thing you do, apply a double standard to the behavior of yourself and the other person, and think about the conflict in polarized, oversimplified ways, the conflict is bound to be destructive to your relationship.

In any conflict situation you and the other person will usually have mixed feelings about each other. On the one hand you will feel hostile and wish that the other person would agree with your position; on the other hand, you will still feel affection for the other person and want to be agreeable to him. When selective perception or distortions in perception operate, it is very easy to fall into a trap where you see only the hostile feelings of the other person and fail to see the positive feelings. This can very easily result in a *self-fulfilling prophecy* in which (1) you assume that the other's feelings are entirely hostile, (2) you take defensive action by either attacking the other person before he can attack you or cutting off contact with the other person, (3) this intensifies the other person's hostility and decreases his positive feelings towards you, and (4) your original, but false assumption is confirmed. Self-fulfilling prophecies are very common in conflict situations, and whenever you become involved in a conflict you should be careful not to fall into their traps.

You may wish to test your understanding of this section by matching the following (answers on p. 225):

_____ 1. Mirror image.

_____ 2. Mote-beam mechanism.

_____ 3. Double standard.

_____ 4. Polarized thinking.

_____ 5. Self-fulfilling prophecy.

a. Everything I do is good; everything you do is bad.

b. What is legitimate for me to do is illegitimate for you to do.

c. I see the mean, underhanded things you do to me but I don't see the mean, underhanded things I do to you.

d. I think I'm right and you're wrong; you think you're right and I'm wrong.

e. I see only your hostile feelings, as I expected, and not your positive ones. I then take defensive action which causes you to be more hostile.

OLD LADY—YOUNG GIRL EXERCISE

The objective of this exercise is to demonstrate how two individuals with different frames of reference can perceive the same event in two different ways. The procedure for the exercise is as follows:

1. Divide into two groups with an equal number of members.

2. Each group receives a picture. One group receives "Picture *A*" (p. 265) and the other group receives "Picture *B*" (p. 267). Each group is asked to write out a description of the person in the picture, including such things as sex, clothing, hair-style, and age of the person in the picture.

3. Each member of the first group is paired with a member of the second group. Each pair is given a copy of "Picture *C*" (p. 269). The two individuals are then asked to negotiate a common description of the person in the picture, including such things as sex, clothing, hair-style, and age.

4. Conduct a discussion in the group as a whole concerning the results of the negotiations. Did you see "Picture *C*" the same way? Once you perceived the picture in one way, was it difficult to see it another way? In conflict situations, what role does your background, previous experience, expectation, and frame of reference have upon how you see your behavior and the behavior of the other person?

5. Review the section on selective perception in Chapter 4. How does the information in that section apply to this situation? How does it apply to most conflict situations?

ENSURING ACCURATE COMMUNICATION

Effective and continued communication is of vital importance in the constructive resolution of conflicts. It is quite common, however, for individuals in a conflict to refuse to communicate with each other when given the opportunity to do so, and when required to communicate they often communicate lies and threats as well as promises and trustworthy statements. Only when communication is aimed at creating an agreement fair to all parties involved is it helpful in resolving a conflict constructively. This means that in communicating with a person you are in conflict with, it is important to keep communication channels open, to communicate promises and trustworthy statements aimed at creating an agreement that is fair to the other person as well as yourself. Sometimes you will find that the other person is not at the moment interested in resolving the conflict. When this is true it is important to include the following elements in your communications to the other person:

1. What your intended behavior to resolve the conflict is going to be.
2. Your expectation as to the other person's response.
3. What you will do if the other person does not behave in the expected way.
4. How friendly, cooperative relationships will be restored after your reaction to the other's violation of your expectations.

In communicating with the other person in a conflict situation, several of the skills that have been emphasized in this book are very helpful. They are:

1. Understanding response.
2. Use of personal and relationship statements in being open about your position, motivations, and feelings.
3. Providing useful, nonevaluative feedback to the other person through constructive confrontations.
4. Communicating acceptance of the other as a person, even when you disagree with his behavior.

In addition, it is important to avoid the use of evaluative responses, threats, lies, indications that you want to "win," and attempts to manipulate the other person; all of these increase the other person's defensiveness, which increases his tendency to misperceive the situation and cut off communication.

You may wish to answer the following questions (answers on p. 225):

1. When is communication in a conflict situation most constructive?
   a. When both parties directly confront each other
   b. When there is someone to mediate the conflict.
   c. When it is well thought out.
   d. When it is aimed at creating a fair agreement.
2. Which of the following are important to include in your communications in a conflict situation?
   a. What your intended behavior to resolve the conflict will be.
   b. How you expect the other person to respond.
   c. What you will do if the other person does not respond in the expected way.
   d. How to restore friendly relationships after the other person has violated your expectations.
   e. All of the above.

ROLE REVERSAL EXERCISE

The primary means of ensuring accurate perception of the conflict situation and of being able to communicate effectively with the other person is to gain as much insight as possible on how the other person perceives the conflict situation. This may be done through a procedure called role reversal. *Role reversal* may be defined as a procedure where one or both of two persons in a conflict present the viewpoint of the other. That is, given that *A* and *B* are in a conflict, *A* presents *B*'s point of view or *B* presents *A*'s point of view, or both. The specific behaviors involved in role reversal are (1) the understanding response while (2) expressing warmth. A variety of research studies have demonstrated that the use of role reversal can eliminate misunderstandings and reduce distortions of the other person's point of view (Johnson, 1966; Johnson and Dustin, 1970).

Whenever you are in a conflict with another person it is of value to engage in role reversal in order to clarify each other's position and feelings. This exercise provides an opportunity to practice role reversal. The procedure is as follows:

1. Pick a current topic of interest on which there are differences of opinion in the group. Then divide the group into half, with each subgroup representing one side of the issue.
2. Each subgroup meets separately for 15 minutes to prepare to represent their side of the issue in negotiations with members of the other subgroup.
3. Each person in the subgroup is paired with a person from the other

subgroup; each pair thus consists of persons representing opposite sides of the issue.

4. In the pair designate the persons *A* and *B*. Person *A* then is given up to five minutes to present his side of the issue. Person *B* then reverses his role by presenting Person *A*'s position as if he were Person *A*.

5. Person *B* then is given up to five minutes to present his side of the issue. Person *A* role reverses.

6. The pair is then given 15 minutes to arrive at a joint agreement on the issue being discussed. During this 15 minutes they must obey the following rule: *Before either can reply to a statement made by the other he must accurately and warmly paraphrase the other's statement to the other's satisfaction.*

7. The group as a whole discuss the impact of role reversal upon their being able to understand and appreciate the other side of the issue. Did role reversal help to reach an agreement? Did it affect how you felt about each other during the negotiations. Did you feel it contributed to reaching a mutually satisfying agreement?

BUILDING A CLIMATE OF TRUST

In dealing constructively with conflicts, it is important to build a climate of trust. There are two major ways to build a climate of trust in dealing with a conflict. The first is to indicate that you trust the other person by making yourself vulnerable through attempts to resolve the conflict constructively. The second is never to exploit the other person's vulnerability. See Chapter 3 for an elaboration of building trust.

STRUCTURING COOPERATIVE SOLUTIONS

Perhaps the surest way of resolving a conflict constructively is to involve yourself and the other person in a situation where you have to cooperate with each other to achieve mutually desired goals. Cooperative interaction means that you and the other person will engage in joint action to accomplish a goal you both desire. Two individuals who both wish to build a sand castle and help each other do so are in cooperative interaction. The members of a football team take cooperative action to win a game. A teacher and a student planning an assignment to maximize the student's learning are in cooperative interaction. Two individuals who wish to deepen their relationship and thus spend time on a joint activity are in cooperative interaction. Any time that you and another person have the same goal and help each other accomplish it you are in co-operative interaction.

Cooperative interaction has very powerful, positive effects upon the relationship between two individuals. Cooperation produces increased liking for one another, increased trust, and a willingness to listen to and be influenced by each other. Friendships are largely based upon cooperation. The development of a fulfilling friendship rests upon the ability of two individuals to define mutual goals (even if the goal is to fall in love) and then cooperate in obtaining them. In a conflict situation, the primary way to ensure a constructive resolution is to work out a cooperative solution to the conflict. Certainly any solution to a conflict decided upon by yourself should include the necessity for cooperative interaction between yourself and the other person. There is no way to overemphasize the importance of ensuring that cooperative interaction in order to achieve mutually desirable goals results from the conflict.

You may wish to answer the following questions (answers on p. 225):

1. What are two ways of building a climate of trust?
   a. Making yourself vulnerable to the other person.
   b. Showing that you like the other person.
   c. Never exploiting the other person's vulnerability.
   d. Showing the other person that you are likeable.
   e. Clobbering the other person with a ball bat.
2. How does cooperative interaction help resolve a conflict?
   a. It takes your mind off the conflict.
   b. It puts both of you in a subservient position.
   c. It increases liking, trust, and willingness to listen to and influence each other.
   d. It increases interaction, thus breaking down perceptual barriers.

DEFINING THE CONFLICT: THE NICKEL AUCTION EXERCISE

This exercise explores the ways in which situations become defined as competitive or cooperative. The procedure for the exercise is as follows:

1. A person designated by the group as the auctioneer has an unlimited supply of nickels. These nickels should be contributed by the group members. The auctioneer plans to auction off the nickels to four members. Four individuals should volunteer to be in the auction.
2. The four volunteers sit in a row. The auctioneer puts a nickel up for auction and each volunteer bids in turn. Bidding is done in units of

1 cent—fractions are not acceptable. The nickel is sold when three of the four volunteers have passed (decided not to bid) in turn. Each time a new nickel is put up for auction the first chance to bid is passed down the line of volunteers; for example, if volunteer A bids first on the first nickel, volunteer B bids first on the second nickel. If members observing the volunteers wish to communicate with them, they are allowed to write notes and pass them to the volunteers.

3. After 20 nickels are sold a group discussion is conducted. Classify the behavior of each volunteer as either basically cooperative or basically competitive. Discuss why the volunteers behaved as they did. What assumptions were they making about the situation?

4. In this situation the volunteers can define the situation as competitive by bidding against each other or they can define it as cooperative by allowing each of the volunteers to buy an equal number of nickels at 1 cent each. A cooperative situation exists if the first bidder bids 1 cent and the other three bidders pass; the next first bidder then bids 1 cent and the others pass, and so on.

5. Discuss in the group why we compete with one another and why we cooperate. Why do we often compete when we would be better off cooperating? Why do we often act as if there is a limited supply of something (such as love) when actually there is an unlimited supply?

How the conflict is defined is one of the most important aspects of a conflict situation. How the causes are defined, how the size is specified, and how the conflict is labeled all affect the management of the conflict. First, you do not want to define the causes of the other person's behavior in a conflict situation in a way that is derogatory to him, such as saying his behavior is motivated by "meanness," "psychopathy," or "racism." Such accusations make the other person highly defensive and angry, thus adding to the difficulty of resolving the conflict in a constructive way. They also contribute to misunderstandings, distrust, feelings of threat, and escalation of the conflict. It is important, however, to define the events leading up to the conflict, especially the event that triggered it. From such a definition the avoidance of triggering events in the future can reduce the possibilities of new conflicts.

The more narrowly the conflict is defined, the easier it is to resolve constructively. Many persons become quite committed to large issues and vague principles when they get into a conflict; this tends to escalate and enlarge the conflict. A teacher, for example, can treat a specific instance of student disobedience as an isolated incident involving one student, or as a sign of deterioration in all students of respect for their elders; the first is often quite easily resolved, the second is unresolvable. Or when two persons disagree, the incident can be dealt with either as a difference of opinion or as a challenge to each of their personalities and basic beliefs. The constructive resolution of conflict is facilitated when the conflict is seen to be as small as possible. Even when a conflict begins on a large level, it is possible to "fractionate" it by reducing its size to the minimum possible.

Labeling the conflict either as a win-or-lose situation, in which one person wins and the other person loses, or alternatively as a joint problem to be solved jointly, has dramatic importance for the constructiveness with which it can be resolved. There are two ways a win-or-lose situation is resolved: either you win or the other person wins. Either way the loser is likely to be resentful and resist implementing any actions that he is supposed to do as a result of the conflict. The loser often feels a great deal of hostility towards the winner and cuts off communication, perceives the winner in unfavorable ways, and tries to "get back at" the winner in the future. Even while the conflict is in process, communication tends to be used to deceive and manipulate the other person, distrust is high, and the two individuals involved tend increasingly to dislike one another.

If the conflict is labeled as a joint problem to be solved, neither you nor the other person will try to "win." In fact, if one person "wins" and the other "loses," something is wrong with the way in which you defined the conflict situation. In a problem-solving situation you and the other person find a creative solution which results in both of you being satisfied. In a problem-solving situation communication is open, trust is developed, and the participants are friendly. Motivation to implement the solution is high on the part of both individuals and no resentment is felt towards the other person. The steps to resolving a problem are as follows:

1. Define the problem. A complete definition of the problem must take into account your behavior and that of the other person and the situation in which the behavior occurs. The definition must be jointly arrived at. In defining the problem it is important for both of you to understand what your differences and your commonalities are; in many conflict situations differences remain hazy and commonalities unknown, both facts contributing to the escalation of the conflict.
   a. How do *you* define the problem? What is your behavior and that of the other person that contributes to or represents the problem?
   b. How does the *other person* define the problem? What does he see as the behavior of yourself and himself which contributes to or represents the problem?

c. How appropriate is your behavior and his to the situation in which the problem occurs?

d. What is the smallest possible definition of the problem?

e. What are the areas of difference or disagreement between the two of you?

f. What are the areas of commonality or agreement between the two of you?

2. Diagnosing causes. Unless you and the other person understand what behavior is acceptable and unacceptable to each other, the conflict is likely to recur in the future. Once the triggering events are understood, it is possible to reduce the possibilities of conflict by avoiding the triggering events.

a. As explicitly as possible, state the other person's behaviors that you find unacceptable in the conflict situation.

b. As explicitly as possible, state your behaviors the other person finds unacceptable in the conflict situation.

c. What events triggered the conflict?

3. Generate possible solutions.

a. What do you need to do to resolve the conflict?

b. What must the other person do to resolve the conflict?

c. What are possible mutually desired goals for the resolution of the conflict?

4. Decide on a mutually acceptable solution. This decision should include an evaluation of the effects of implementing each possible solution and an understanding of the need for cooperative interaction to take place as a result of the solution being implemented.

a. What is the outcome of implementing each possible solution?

b. What cooperative interaction will take place as a result of each solution being implemented?

c. What solution do the two of you feel will be most constructive?

5. Implement the solution.

6. Evaluate whether the solution solved the problem. If it did not, repeat all of the above steps. How can you tell if the implemented solution worked or did not work?

You may wish to answer the following questions (answers on p. 225):

True   False   1. Labeling the other person's behavior helps resolve a conflict.

True   False   2. Defining the conflict is one of the most important aspects of resolving it.

True   False   3. Defining the triggering events in a conflict helps avoid future conflicts.

True   False   4. The larger the conflict is defined, the easier it is to resolve it constructively.

True   False   5. It is helpful to identify the winner and the loser in a conflict.

EXERCISE IN RESOLVING CONFLICTS CONSTRUCTIVELY

The following exercise provides an opportunity to practice resolving a conflict constructively. Think of a conflict you are having with another person. If possible, ask the other person to help you answer the questions below; if the other person participates, any answer must be agreed upon by the two of you. If the other person cannot or will not participate, answer the following questions to the best of your ability.

1. How do you define the problem between yourself and the other person?

_____

_____

_____

_____

2. How does the other person define the problem?

_____

_____

_____

_____

3. What behavior of yourself contributes to or represents the problem?

_____

_____

_____

_____

4. What behavior of the other person contributes to or represents the problem?

_____

_____

_____

_____

5. What is the situation in which the above behaviors occur?

_____

_____

_____

_____

6. What is the smallest way possible to define the problem?

_____

_____

_____

_____

7. What are the areas of difference or disagreement between the two of you?

_____

_____

_____

_____

8. What are the areas of commonality or agreement between the two of you?

_____

_____

_____

_____

9. As explicitly as possible, state the other person's behaviors that you find unacceptable in the conflict situation.

_____

_____

_____

_____

10. As explicitly as possible, state your behaviors that the other person finds unacceptable in the conflict situation.

_____

_____

_____

_____

11. What events triggered the conflict?

_____

_____

_____

_____

12. In answering the above questions, we have avoided:

_____ a. Mirror image.

_____ b. Mote-beam mechanism.

_____ c. Double standard.

_____ d. Polarized thinking.

_____ e. Negative self-fulfilling prophecies.

_____ f. Cutting off or refusing to communicate.

_____ g. Using communication to deceive, manipulate, threaten or coerce.

13. In answering the above questions we have used:

_____ a. Personal statements.

_____ b. Relationship statements.

_____ c. Understanding response.

_____ d. Role reversal.

_____ e. Constructive confrontation.

_____ f. Communication of acceptance.

_____ g. Building of trust.

14. What are the things you need to do in order to resolve the conflict?

_____

_____

_____

_____

15. What are the things the other person needs to do to resolve the conflict?

_____

_____

_____

_____

16. What are possible mutually desired goals which the two of you could cooperate in achieving in order to resolve the conflict?

_____

_____

_____

_____

17. What are your strengths you could utilize to resolve the conflict?

_____

_____

_____

_____

18. What are the other person's strengths he could utilize to resolve the conflict?

_____

_____

_____

_____

19. How will the two of you know if the conflict has been resolved?

_____

_____

_____

_____

CHECKLIST OF SKILLS

1. In dealing with an interpersonal conflict, I have mastered the following:

   _____ An awareness of my personal style of conflict management.

   _____ Avoiding common misperceptions which intensify the conflict.

   _____ Ensuring accurate communication aimed at reaching an agreement which is fair to both myself and the other person.

   _____ Building a climate of trust.

   _____ Structuring cooperative solutions.

   _____ Ensuring a constructive definition of the conflict.

2. I need more work on the following:

   _____ An awareness of my personal style of conflict management.

   _____ Avoiding common misperceptions which intensify the conflict.

   _____ Ensuring accurate communication aimed at reaching an agreement which is fair to both myself and the other person.

   _____ Building a climate of trust.

   _____ Structuring cooperative solutions.

   _____ Ensuring a constructive definition of the conflict.

ANSWERS

Page 204: 1: c; 2: c; 3: b, c, e
Page 212: 1: d; 2: c; 3: b; 4: a; 5: e
Page 214: 1: d; 2: e
Page 216: 1: a, c; 2: c
Pages 219–220: 1: False; 2: True; 3: True; 4: False; 5: False

Epilogue

Interpersonal skills are vital for interpersonal effectiveness and self-actualization. As was noted in the first chapter, there is no way to over-emphasize the importance of interpersonal skills in our daily lives. We are not born with these skills, they must be developed. You have now completed a variety of experiences aimed at improving your interpersonal skills. Hopefully you are now more self-aware, self-accepting, and self-disclosing. You have had a variety of experiences in building trust, in giving and receiving constructive feedback, and in communicating ideas and feelings accurately and unambiguously. You have had practice in expressing support and acceptance to other individuals, confronting other people, and modeling appropriate behavior. You have been ex-posed to ways of reinforcing both your own and other person's behavior. You have had practice in handling conflicts constructively. You may find that you wish to repeat many of the exercises and reread much of the material in this book in order to learn how to utilize it fully in your relationships with other individuals. There is, however, a concluding exercise which may be helpful in applying the material covered in this book to your relationships.

RELATIONSHIP SURVEY

The objectives of this exercise are to increase your awareness of the qualities of meaningful relationships in your life and to commit you to applying the skills and insights you have gained from this book to increase the meaningfulness of your present relationships. You will need a large sheet of newsprint and a magic-marker for the exercise. The procedure for the exercise is as follows:

1. Write your name at the top of the newsprint and divide it into two columns. On one side write in four of your relationships that you value highly and on the other side write in what it is that you value about the relationship. These could be relationships you are presently involved in or ones you have had in the past.

2. In the group as a whole share this information. This provides an opportunity for you to practice self-disclosure and listening skills. After each person has shared his information, the group should suggest what they perceive as the essential qualities of a meaningful relationship for that person. The person should then write down the suggestions of the group in the appropriate column of the newsprint.

3. Divide into trios. Within the trio each person reviews his strengths and the skills and insights he has learned from this book. He then picks several of the relationships he is now involved in and sets a series of goals concerning how he will behave in order to increase their meaningfulness. Discuss the goals within the trio. Make sure they conform to the criteria for setting objectives discussed in Chapter 10.

4. Address an envelope to yourself. Plan how you will behave in the next six months to accomplish the goals you have just set. Write a letter to yourself specifying your goals and your behavior in the relationships selected during the next six months. Seal the letter. Open it six months from today.

REFERENCES

Bierman, R. Dimension for interpersonal facilitation in psychotherapy in child development. *Psychological Bulletin,* 1969, **72**, 338–352.

Deutch, M. Cooperation and trust: Some theoretical notes. In M. R. Jones (Ed.), *Nebraska Symposium on Motivation.* Lincoln: University of Nebraska Press, 1962, pp. 275–319.

Frost, R. *Revelation. Complete Poems of Robert Frost.* New York: Holt, Rinehart, and Winston, 1964, p. 27.

Hamachek, D. E. *Encounters with The Self.* New York: Holt, Rinehart, and Winston, 1971.

Harris, T. A. *I'm OK—You're OK.* New York: Harper & Row, Publishers, 1967.

Johnson, D. W. The use of role reversal in intergroup competition. *Journal of Personality and Social Psychology,* 1967, **7,** 135–141.

Johnson, D. W. *The Social Psychology of Education.* New York: Holt, Rinehart, and Winston, 1970.

Johnson, D. W. The effects of warmth of interaction, accuracy of understanding, and the proposal of compromises on the listener's behavior. *Journal of Counseling Psychology,* 1971, **18,** 207–216.

Johnson, D. W. The effects of expressing warmth and anger upon the actor and the listener. *Journal of Counseling Psychology,* 1971, **18,** 571–578.

Johnson, D. W. The effectiveness of role reversal: the actor or the listener. *Psychological Reports,* 1971, **28,** 275–282.

Johnson, D. W. *Readings in Humanistic Social Psychology.* Philadelphia, Pa.: Lippincott, 1972.

Johnson, D. W., & Dustin, R. The initiation of cooperation through role reversal. *Journal of Social Psychology,* 1970, **82,** 193–203.

Johnson, D. W., & Lewicki, R. J. The initiation of superordinate goals. *Journal of Applied Behavioral Science,* 1969, **5,** 9–24.

Jourard, S. *The Transparent Self.* New York: Van Nostrand Reinhold Co., 1964.

Luce, R. D., & Raiffa, H. *Games and Decisions.* New York: John Wiley & Sons, 1957

Luft, J. *Of Human Interaction.* Palo Alto, Cal.: National Press, 1969.

McCroskey, J. C., Larson, C. E. & Knapp, M. L. *Introduction to Interpersonal Communication.* Englewood Cliffs, N.J.: Prentice-Hall, Inc., 1971.

Porter, E. H., Jr. *Therapeutic Counseling.* Boston: Houghton Mifflin Company, 1950.

Rogers, C. R. *Client-centered Therapy.* Boston: Houghton Mifflin Company, 1951.

Rogers, C. R. & Roethlisberger, F. J. Barriers and gateways to communication. *Harvard Business Review,* July–August, 1952, 28–35.

Rogers, C. R. Dealing with psychological tensions. *Journal of Applied Behavioral Science,* 1965, **1,** (1), 6–25.

Strupp, H. H., & Bergin, A. E. Some empirical and conceptual bases for coordinated research in psychotherapy: A critical review of issues, trends, and evidence. *International Journal of Psychiatry,* 1969, **7,** 18–90.

Truax, C. B., & Carkhuff, R. R. *Toward Effective Counseling and Psychotherapy: Training and Practice.* Chicago: Aldine Publishing Co., 1967.

Watson, G., & Johnson, D. W. *Social Psychology: Issues and Insights* (2d ed.). Philadelphia, Pa.: Lippincott, 1972.

FRIENDSHIP RELATIONS SURVEY ANSWER SHEET

	A	*B*
1.	_____	_____
2.	_____	_____
3.	_____	_____
4.	_____	_____
5.	_____	_____
6.	_____	_____
7.	_____	_____
8.	_____	_____
9.	_____	_____
10.	_____	_____
11.	_____	_____
12.	_____	_____
13.	_____	_____
14.	_____	_____
15.	_____	_____
16.	_____	_____
17.	_____	_____
18.	_____	_____
19.	_____	_____
20.	_____	_____

FRIENDSHIP RELATIONS SURVEY ANSWER KEY

In the Friendship Relations Survey there are ten questions which deal with your receptivity to feedback from friends and ten questions which are concerned with your willingness to self-disclose, be open, or give feedback to your friends. Transfer your scores from the "Survey Answer Sheet" to this "Survey Answer Key." Add the scores in the "receptivity to feedback" column; then add the scores in the "willingness to self-disclose" column. Do not count any points for the alternatives which measure neither receptivity to feedback nor willingness to self-disclose.

Receptivity to Feedback	Willingness to Self-Disclose
2. B _____	1. A _____
3. A _____	4. B _____
5. A _____	6. B _____
7. A _____	9. B _____
8. B _____	11. B _____
10. B _____	13. A _____
12. B _____	15. A _____
14. B _____	17. B _____
16. A _____	18. B _____
20. A _____	19. B _____
Total: _____	Total: _____

On the "Friendship Relations Survey Summary Sheet," p. 235, add the totals for "receptivity to feedback" to the total points for "willingness to self-disclose" to arrive at an index of interpersonal risk-taking, which is relevant to Chapter 3.

FRIENDSHIP RELATIONS SURVEY SUMMARY SHEET

	Your Scores	*Group* *Average Scores*
Receptivity to Feedback:		
Willingness to Self-Disclose:	(+)	(+)
Interpersonal Risk-Taking:		

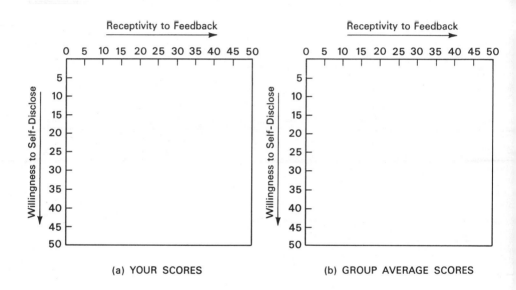

(a) YOUR SCORES   (b) GROUP AVERAGE SCORES

Draw horizontal and vertical lines through your scores—part a, above—and the group's receptivity to feedback and willingness to self-disclose—part b, above. The results should look like the Johari Window.

RECORD SHEET: PRISONER'S DILEMMA GAME

	Your Choice	Other's Choice	Your Gain or Loss	Your Total	Other's Gain or Loss	Other's Total
1.						
2.						
3.						
4.						
5.						
6.						
7.						
8.						
9.						
10.						
11.						
12.						
13.						
14.						
15.						
16.						
17.						
18.						
19.						
20.						

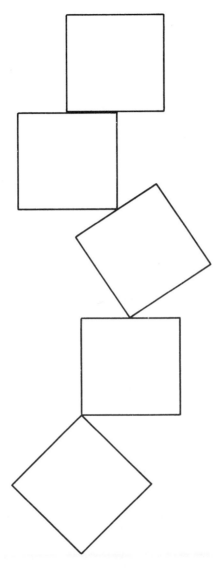

Instructions: The sender is to study the figures above. With his back to the group, he is to instruct the members of the group how to draw them. He should begin with the top square and describe each in succession, taking particular note of the placement relationship of each to the preceding one. No questions are allowed.

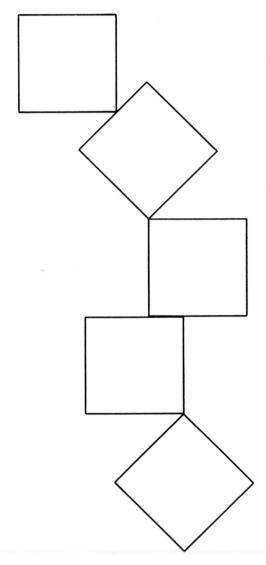

Instructions: The sender is to study the figures above. Facing the group, he is to instruct the members how to draw them. He should begin with the top square and describe each in succession, taking particular note of the placement relationship of each to the preceding one. He should answer all questions from participants and repeat his descriptions if necessary.

OBSERVATION SHEET FOR INEFFECTIVE COMMUNICATION

1. The receiver fails to listen to the message:

   _____

   _____

2. The receiver only listens to part of the message in order to say what he wants to say rather than respond fully to the message:

   _____

   _____

3. The receiver distorts the message to conform with his expectations of what he thought the sender was going to say:

   _____

   _____

4. The receiver is listening in order to make judgments and evaluations of the sender, thus making the sender defensive and guarded in formulating the message:

   _____

   _____

5. The receiver understood the words of the message but not the underlying meaning:

   _____

   _____

6. The sender uses general pronouns and nouns to refer to his own feelings and ideas:

   _____

   _____

7. Other ineffective communication behaviors:

   _____

   _____

OBSERVATION SHEET FOR EFFECTIVE COMMUNICATION BEHAVIOR

1. The receiver paraphrases the sender's remarks:

_____

_____

2. The receiver checks out the meaning of the sender's remarks:

_____

_____

3. The receiver does not give evaluations or judgments about the sender's remarks:

_____

_____

4. The receiver keeps his interpretation of the sender's remarks tentative until he checks it out with the sender:

_____

_____

5. The receiver focused upon the meaning of the message, not the specific words:

_____

_____

6. The sender used personal statements:

_____

_____

7. The sender used relationship statements:

_____

_____

8. Other effective communication behaviors:

_____

_____

ANSWER SHEET I: IDENTIFYING PERSONAL RESPONSES

Read the 12 statements and circle on this answer sheet the response which best represents what you would personally say to the speaker if you were trying to form a close relationship with him and help him solve his problems.

1.	1 : 2 : 3 : 4 : 5
2.	1 : 2 : 3 : 4 : 5
3.	1 : 2 : 3 : 4 : 5
4.	1 : 2 : 3 : 4 : 5
5.	1 : 2 : 3 : 4 : 5
6.	1 : 2 : 3 : 4 : 5
7.	1 : 2 : 3 : 4 : 5
8.	1 : 2 : 3 : 4 : 5
9.	1 : 2 : 3 : 4 : 5
10.	1 : 2 : 3 : 4 : 5
11.	1 : 2 : 3 : 4 : 5
12.	1 : 2 : 3 : 4 : 5

Response	Frequency
E	_____
I	_____
S	_____
P	_____
U	_____

ANSWER SHEET II: IDENTIFYING THE INTENT OF A RESPONSE

Study the sheet on which the five basic intents underlying the responses to the problems presented in the questionnaire are discussed (p. 125). Then go back through the questionnaire and classify the responses to each problem according to the five categories. Read each of the twelve statements of a problem and identify the intent underlying each of the alternative responses by marking a *P* for probing, *I* for interpretative, *E* for evaluative, *S* for supportive, and *U* for understanding.

Item	1	2	3	4	5
1.					
2.					
3.					
4.					
5.					
6.					
7.					
8.					
9.					
10.					
11.					
12.					

SCORING KEY FOR IDENTIFYING THE INTENT OF A RESPONSE

When you have completed Answer Sheet II, use this scoring key to score the type of responses you personally gave for each item (Answer Sheet I). Then divide into groups of three, score the accuracy with which you correctly identified the different response for each item (Answer Sheet II), and discuss each answer in your group of three until everyone understands it.

Item	1	2	3	4	5
1.	I	S	E	U	P
2.	E	U	I	P	S
3.	U	I	P	S	E
4.	P	U	E	S	I
5.	S	P	U	I	E
6.	P	U	I	E	S
7.	E	I	P	S	U
8.	S	E	U	P	I
9.	U	P	E	S	I
10.	P	U	E	S	I
11.	I	E	S	U	P
12.	U	P	S	E	I

ANSWER SHEET III: IDENTIFYING PERSONAL RESPONSES

Read the nine statements and mark on this answer sheet the response which best represents what you would personally say to the speaker if you were trying to form a close personal friendship with him and help him solve his problems.

13.	1	:	2	:	3	:	4
14.	1	:	2	:	3	:	4
15.	1	:	2	:	3	:	4
16.	1	:	2	:	3	:	4
17.	1	:	2	:	3	:	4
18.	1	:	2	:	3	:	4
19.	1	:	2	:	3	:	4
20.	1	:	2	:	3	:	4
21.	1	:	2	:	3	:	4

Response	Frequency
A	_____
S	_____
P	_____
I	_____

ANSWER SHEET IV: IDENTIFYING THE PHRASING
OF UNDERSTANDING RESPONSES

Study the sheet on which the four different phrasings of understanding responses are discussed. Then read each of the nine statements and identify the category of each understanding response by: I = identical content, P = paraphrasing content, S = shallow or partial meaning, and A = additional meaning.

Item	1	2	3	4
13.				
14.				
15.				
16.				
17.				
18.				
19.				
20.				
21.				

SCORING KEY FOR THE PHRASING OF UNDERSTANDING RESPONSES

When you have completed "Answer Sheet IV," use this scoring key to score the type of phrasing you personally gave for each item ("Answer Sheet III.") Then divide into groups of three, score the accuracy with which you correctly identified the different types of phrasing for each item (Answer Sheet IV), and discuss each answer in your group until everyone understands it.

Item	1	2	3	4
13.	I	A	P	S
14.	S	I	P	A
15.	A	S	I	P
16.	P	A	S	I
17.	I	P	A	S
18.	P	S	A	I
19.	A	P	I	S
20.	P	I	S	A
21.	I	S	A	P

OBSERVATION SHEET

Listening with understanding	*Person 1*	*Person 2*
Paraphrased other's feelings and ideas in one's own words	————	————
Did not indicate approval or disapproval	————	————
Depth of response was appropriate	————	————
Did not add or subtract meaning	————	————
Did not change the feeling tone	————	————
Negotiated for meaning	————	————
Language was understandable and appropriate	————	————
Perception check for other's feelings	————	————

Expression of warmth	*Person 1*	*Person 2*
Direct description of own feelings	————	————
Tone of voice	————	————
Facial expression	————	————
Posture	————	————
Eye contact	————	————
Touching	————	————
Gestures	————	————
Spatial distance	————	————
Congruence among verbal, nonverbal, and tacit expressions of feelings	————	————

OBSERVATION SHEET

In the spaces below, count the number of times the confronter used the skills involved in constructive confrontation.

	Practicing Confrontations	*Role-Playing Confrontations*
Personal statements	_____	_____
Relationship statements	_____	_____
Behavior-description statements	_____	_____
Description-of-own-feeling statements	_____	_____
Understanding response	_____	_____
Perception-check-of-other's-feelings statements	_____	_____
Interpretative response	_____	_____
Constructive feedback	_____	_____

RECORD SHEET

	Number of Times Other Person Engaged in Behavior to Be Increased	Number of Times I Engaged in a Strengthening Consequence
Day One		
Day Two		
Day Three		
Day Four		
Day Five		
Day Six		
Day Seven		

NOTES

NOTES

NOTES

NOTES

DATE DUE			
JAN 3 1978		AUG 6 1983	
MAY 13 1978		MAR 01 1984	
MAY 17 1978			
DEC 1 1978		SEP 25 1984	
JUL 05 1979			
OCT 3 0 1980		JUN 12 1985	
MAY 03 1981		MAR 16 1988	
SEP 23 1981			
APR 3 1982		JUN 2 0 1994	
APR 23 1982		NOV 0 6 1999	